Principals and Teachers Can't Do It All

Principals and Teachers Can't Do It All

Other Factors That Impact the Success of Students and Schools

Charles A. Bonnici

ROWMAN & LITTLEFIELD
Lanham • Boulder • New York • London

Published by Rowman & Littlefield
An imprint of The Rowman & Littlefield Publishing Group, Inc.
4501 Forbes Boulevard, Suite 200, Lanham, Maryland 20706
www.rowman.com

6 Tinworth Street, London, SE11 5AL, United Kingdom

Copyright © 2021 by Charles A. Bonnici

All rights reserved. No part of this book may be reproduced in any form or by any electronic or mechanical means, including information storage and retrieval systems, without written permission from the publisher, except by a reviewer who may quote passages in a review.

British Library Cataloguing in Publication Information Available

Library of Congress Cataloging-in-Publication Data

Names: Bonnici, Charles A., 1948– author.
Title: Principals and teachers can't do it all : other factors that impact the success of students and schools / Charles A. Bonnici.
Description: Lanham : Rowman & Littlefield, [2021] | Includes bibliographical references. | Summary: "After exploring the other factors impacting on school success, this book looks at teachers and principals, not from the viewpoint of what they can do, but the viewpoint of their limitations."—Provided by publisher.
Identifiers: LCCN 2020035498 (print) | LCCN 2020035499 (ebook) | ISBN 9781475857108 (cloth) | ISBN 9781475857115 (paperback) | ISBN 9781475857122 (epub)
Subjects: LCSH: Educational evaluation—United States. | School improvement programs—United States. | Academic achievement—United States. | Educational leadership—United States. | School principals—United States. | Teachers—United States.
Classification: LCC LB2822.75 .B66 2021 (print) | LCC LB2822.75 (ebook) | DDC 371.2/07—dc23
LC record available at https://lccn.loc.gov/2020035498
LC ebook record available at https://lccn.loc.gov/2020035499

For my grandchildren, the joys of my later years and, like all our grandchildren, our hope for the future of our country and this world: Alexander Joaquin (8th grade), Gwenhwyfar Rayne (3rd grade), and Isolde Wren (1st grade).

Contents

Foreword	ix
Preface	xiii
Acknowledgments	xvii
Introduction	xix
1 Money	1
2 "The Powers That Be"	19
3 The School Building	35
4 Parents	47
5 Students	59
6 The Support Staff and a Foray into Bargaining Agreements	77
7 Teachers	91
8 Principals	111
Bibliography	129
About the Author	137

Foreword

During this brief period of respite from the school reform movement, when we educators can take a breath from constantly being second-guessed, I find myself wondering what will come next in the education zeitgeist. Following the rise of the grassroots anti-testing movement and then a pandemic that, while engendering some nostalgia for the "good old days," must ultimately result in monumental change, career educators cannot help but contemplate a vision of the future.

A career educator is exactly what I so proudly am. I cannot imagine a profession more honorable, rewarding, and consequential. For nearly thirty-four years, I've served as a teacher, assistant principal, principal, and union leader. As president of The Council of School Supervisors and Administrators, Local 1: American Federation of School Administrators, AFL-CIO, I have the privilege of serving thousands of school leaders whose mission in life is to foster the most fruitful possible instructional environment for teachers and students.

Experience gives one the insight to almost instantly recognize a craftsman. So, when I first encountered Charles A. Bonnici at union headquarters, I knew he was a veteran of the education wars, a survivor, and a soldier whose entire life had been devoted to educating children in our public schools. Charlie also turned out to be one of those people who educates the educators. He is a top consultant to our union's professional development arm, The Educational Leadership Institute (ELI). ELI delivers practical, relevant, and essential professional development for today's school leaders. He has also mentored many of our new principals and assistant principals.

Charles Bonnici has never tired of his vocation. Some fifty years ago, he started out as a teacher of English at New York's Louis D. Brandeis High School, which at the time was an extremely large general curriculum high school in Manhattan. He went on to become an assistant principal for more than ten years at the High School of Fashion Industries, another sizable Manhattan secondary school, a CTE school, with a focus on careers in the fashion industry. He became its principal for even longer. In spirit, Charlie never left the classroom but went on to develop and teach courses in educational leadership at New York's Pace University, from "The Fundamentals of Educational Leadership" to "Strategic Planning for Educational Leaders."

To this day, he is devoted to his profession, consulting for our ELI and lecturing on subjects as varied as urban education and the Common Core Standards. He also publishes widely on the priorities of school leadership and creating a leadership style, and he develops handbooks for teachers and administrators. With that breadth of knowledge and expertise, he is perfectly suited to write about the whole gestalt of the K–12 educational experience, and that is what he has done in his latest book, *Principals and Teachers Can't Do It All: Other Factors That Impact the Success of Students and Schools*. For the sake of brevity, I will refer to this new work as *Can't Do It All*.

In reading this overview of modern and contemporary schools, I would suggest you follow a nonlinear path, detouring where curiosity and need lead you. Although, by and large, Charlie writes about public schools, his observations and conclusions are generally applicable to all kinds of schools. The comprehensive topics include the entities that govern schools; funding and budget; the physical plant itself; and, most importantly, the living beings, the lifeblood of every school: children; parents; teachers; administrators; guidance counselors; and clerical, support, and custodial staff. No one is overlooked because, in fact, as all school leaders know, each and every individual forms the beating heart of the community that we call "school."

Another piece of advice I would offer you when reading *Can't Do It All* is to consider one of Charles Bonnici's fundamental premises, which is that, for too many years, backwards thinking has determined how schools are viewed in society. There has been an assumption, a credo, if you will, of the somewhat languishing reform movement that promulgates the belief that "fixing" our schools will "fix" our society. In Charlie's view, the reverse is true. He believes that, although elected officials, school districts, and even parents can crunch the numbers to rate teachers, school leaders, and the schools overall, their conclusions are largely fallacious and do not move schools forward.

Often, it is quite the contrary. The statistics and analytics unreliably measure very narrow outcomes and fail to take into account key factors of family and community, which have proven to be reliable predictors of standardized test scores. Until poverty and income inequality can at least be substantially mitigated, optimum results for all students, as currently measured, is unlikely to be achieved nationwide. In Charlie's view, those two metrics of poverty and income inequality are moving more than ever in the wrong direction and encompassing an increasing number of young people. Perhaps, we should focus on schools and society simultaneously, and perhaps we need to find a better way to measure what we truly value, rather than being forced to value what statisticians have been able to somewhat objectively measure.

Even if you do not accept Charlie's view of social reality, you will probably find that he offers some sound strategies for creating a successful school system within the framework of an imperfect society. We must do all we can to attract and retain teachers, the heroes of our education system, by boosting their salaries and prestige; to attract and increase the number of guidance counselors, the experts at detecting what inspires or stymies our students; and to cross-pollinate the training of teachers and counselors.

When it comes to school leaders, the wizards and choreographers who assemble all the bits and pieces that make up our schools, he suggests that they are our greatest hope and cites the 2019 Pew Research Center study that "made headlines proclaiming that of the many professions studied, K–12 principals were the most trusted by Americans, coming in ahead of police officers, military leaders and religious leaders." And he devises strategies for compensating school leaders with salaries commensurate with the high level of faith the public seems to have in their professionalism.

I applaud Charles A. Bonnici for daring to dive into this deep, sober examination and analysis of our public schools. He makes a significant contribution to understanding the extremely complex institutions that contribute more than any other to the very fabric of society.

Mark F. Cannizzaro
President, Council of School
Supervisors and Administrators
New York City

Preface

How can we best evaluate schools, teachers, and students? How can we know that a school is doing well? What makes a school successful?

These questions are on the lips of superintendents and political leaders and in the headlines of newspapers. In today's world the answer is test students and use test results to evaluate the success of teachers, principals, and schools. This despite the truth known to every educator: More and more testing is not the answer and may diminish learning.

The current methods of school evaluation are flawed because they minimize or ignore critical factors that impact on the success of students and schools. I am writing this book to expand the conversation by looking at these additional factors. I will draw upon research, anecdotes, and my perspective of fifty years as an educator.

To set the stage for this book, we need to look at the past.

In the 17th century, in the first schools in the Massachusetts Bay Colony, success was easy to measure: students would "graduate" able to read the Bible. Moving into the 18th and early 19th centuries, "good citizenship" became an additional criteria: students would be literate enough to vote intelligently. The multitude of letters from Civil War soldiers from all walks of life indicates that the literacy rate was relatively high mid-19th century.

As the industrial revolution expanded, helping students become productive members of society and good workers were added as criteria. One need not advance much beyond elementary school to be able to read, do sums, and earn a living. During the Great Depression, when everyone needed to earn even a meager income, having children complete elementary school was difficult for the majority of families.

World War II changed everything. Getting a good education became the key to the future, to a world beyond farm and factory jobs. The G.I. Bill brought millions of veterans into higher education. As the economy of the country shifted from manufacturing to service and data, the thrust for educational systems to prepare students for college became more and more urgent. The Common Core Standards is an attempt to ensure that education in every state is rigorous enough to do just that.

How can you ensure students are prepared for college? You take the concept of college entry testing and move it further and further back until students are tested in every subject on multiple grade levels. Then, you hire statisticians to create complicated metrics and use the results of these tests to evaluate schools, teachers, and principals. Wiggins never imagined this type of backward design!

Test results and student outcomes cannot be the sole criteria used for these evaluations. They are but two of several variables. To ignore the other factors that contribute to the success or failure of a school is like judging the esthetics of a painting by looking at less than a quarter of the canvas. The other elements were not always ignored. Some were even the preferred criteria in the not so distant past.

When I began teaching in an inner city school in the early 1970s, there was a feeling that teachers faced an overwhelming task, fighting against a negative tide of poverty, poor medical care, societal ills, and poor parental child-rearing practices in the preschool years. Most teachers knew that despite this, they could make a difference in the lives of many (but not all) children in their classrooms.

The government, through LBJ's Great Society programs, tried to address these issues. There was a two-prong solution: address societal problems and improve the schools. Medicare, Medicaid, and welfare reform attacked societal issues. The Elementary and Secondary Education Act (which included Title I funding), Head Start, the College Bound Program, and other initiatives supported the schools.

Since then many of the social programs have been eviscerated or eliminated while some school support programs continue. The idea that if you can change society you can improve student outcomes became if you can change the schools, you can fix society. This false notion continues to plague schools today.

Another factor was added into the mix in the late 1980s and early 1990s: realization of the importance of the role of school leaders, particularly principals. Money spent by districts to support schools was decentralized into the hands of building principals to create educational programs meeting the needs of their students. Principals had always wanted more authority and autonomy, but it often came with a price, the dismantling of district support systems. With the advent of the Common Core Standards, much of this autonomy was lost as districts reasserted their power and dictated methods of implementation.

Creeping in at the same time was a distrust of school leaders and teachers that has culminated in our current craze for tests. Let me give an example. When I was a high school principal in New York City, students needed to earn a specified number of credits in each subject area and pass a minimum of five state mandated examinations: Global Studies, American History and Government, English, Living Environment, and Mathematics. The testing time frame was flexible. Some schools doubled social studies periods in the ninth year and gave the Global exam at the end of the freshman year.

My staff and I devised programs for individual students depending on their needs when they entered high school. The subject area supervisors reviewed each student's middle school record, standardized test results, and our own school-devised placement examinations to determine which class or classes they needed in the ninth year.

The mathematics chair, for example, would determine if a student would need two, three, or four semesters to be prepared for the one required mathematics examination. Further, he determined if a student needed to be placed in an extra remedial class and/or a reduced size regular math class.

Placement was more complicated than the previous paragraphs would indicate. Transcripts and tests were tempered by teacher input. Ninth year classes on different levels were paralleled to permit class transfers based on teacher evaluations given during the first few weeks in September.

My leadership staff and I created a priority for supplemental classes for students with multiple needs because we felt it was counterproductive to give students more than one remedial class and significantly longer school days. And, of course, funding for such classes was limited.

We recognized that students entered high school at different levels and that each needed an individualized program to address their needs. We had no Common Core, so we had more curricular flexibility and more accountability. While teachers were not held accountable for test results, the principal and assistant principals were. We used backward design before Wiggins wrote about it.

As a new AP/English Supervision in 1980, I had my staff work with me to design a cohesive curriculum from ninth grade to eleventh grade to prepare students for the required exam administered at the end of the junior year. We did not want to detract from a child's education by devoting the 11th year to test prep. From the first course in ninth year, students began learning the skills they would need to succeed on the exam, seamlessly woven into the fabric of a curriculum that stressed reading, writing, listening, and speaking.

We looked ahead. We wanted to better prepare students for the SATs, and so we incorporated the close reading of nonfiction articles into instruction (many aspects of the Common Core are not new). Teachers tried to find readings related to the literature being covered. For example, a local newspaper reported that people had seen a Loch Ness type monster in the Hudson River. A reading of the article became the motivation (now called "the hook") for a reading and discussion of Ray Bradbury's short story, "The Fog Horn."

As a principal, I asked all my subject area supervisors to create the same kind of backward design to ensure that test prep would not detract from instruction. The challenge for all staff was to provide students with a real education to prepare them for college, career, and life while at the same time giving them the tools to pass required examinations and earn a diploma.

Our goal was simple: to provide supports, individualized programs, and curricula so that at least 80% of students passed each examination on the first attempt. Those who succeeded could take advanced classes and electives, academic or occupational; those who did not would have coursework to help them succeed on the next attempt. This coursework was mainly test prep, but as first attempt results improved, it affected fewer and fewer students.

The leadership and staff of the school were trusted to create programs and adapt state curricular outlines to meet the needs of students and improve student outcomes. There is no such trust today. Instead, there is the overtesting of students, more test preparation, and less real instruction. Student outcomes are not significantly improving, test ratings are questionable, evaluation metrics incomprehensible, and the incidences of cheating increasing. Perhaps education by statistics is not the answer for determining school success.

Understanding that teachers and principals cannot do it all is important. A well-educated citizenship will positively impact on society. It is doubtful this can be achieved without addressing the many ills of society, particularly the number of people living at or below the poverty level and the widening gap between the haves and have-nots. Schools are not the answer to society's problems, only one of the strategies for addressing them.

Acknowledgments

This book was percolating in my brain for several years. My thanks to Rowman editor Tom Koerner for encouraging me to finally write it and to Carlie Wall for helping me with technical information. Thanks also to Lara Hahn, who provided invaluable assistance with the editing process.

While most of the anecdotes included have been drawn from my fifty years of experience, many of my colleagues at the Executive Leadership Institute and others I have worked with over the years provided me with ideas and stories, especially Gerard Beirne, Frank Brancato, Mitch Pinsky, Thomas Conway, Tina Houck, Heather Page, and Ron Weiss. Thanks also to my daughter, Danielle, a New York City teacher and parent of two girls in public elementary schools, and my son, Stephen, whose son attends a public middle school in Melbourne, Florida.

Thanks to my colleagues who gave up their time to read and review the book, Eloise Messineo, John Lee, and Gerard Berine.

A very special thank you to Mark Cannizzaro, who, while supporting the school leaders of New York City through the brave new world of distance learning and distance supervision during the COVID-19 pandemic, found time to write the thoughtful foreword to this book.

My wife, Christine, is my first editor, who ensures that I submit the cleanest possible copy. She also allowed me to monopolize our computer (after she bought her own tablet) and gave me countless hours of "back of the head" time to complete this book. She has been my better half throughout my entire career, always ready to help with everything from serving as hostess at school events, to helping me deal with those difficult times every principal has, to getting me started on my most recent career as educational writer. How can you thank someone for almost fifty years of love and devotion?

Introduction

This is not the book I intended to write.

As I entered my fiftieth year as an educator—teacher, assistant principal, college instructor and program coordinator, and now educational consultant—I wanted to draw upon my experience and expertise to discuss the factors that lead to a school's success. Over the past four years, I had written sections of several chapters, but an actual book was not a top priority. Then, I realized that I had written half the book—or so I thought.

I decided to check some of my ideas using the internet and opened a digital Pandora's Box. One Google search led to another. I found a mountain of sites, sources, and statistics to sift through. Much of my planned anecdotal book became research based. The data I mined provided an unexpected theme and first chapter, "Money," but not in the traditional sense where more money for education equals better results for schools and students. The issue is far more complex.

I intended to give short shrift to teachers and principals because so much has been written about their importance to the success of students and schools. The information I uncovered led me to expand these chapters, looking at these key players from a different perspective. I home in on the impact of low salaries, lack of autonomy, and diminishing prestige. I delineate what they actually can and cannot do to help children and improve schools.

Chapter 1 is all about numbers, which seems fitting in today's world of education by statistics. Politicians, parents, and school districts assume there is a cause and effect relationship between school supervision, instruction, and student achievement. They crunch numbers to rate teachers, principals, and schools. Their thinking is skewed. The statistics and analytics fail to incorporate key factors that lead to students' and schools' successes or failures. They discount societal factors that severely limit what teachers and school leaders can accomplish. This book will correct this.

Think of the schema of this book as a funnel, beginning with the wider end of a global perspective, moving along past "the powers that be," the school building, parents, students, nonpedagogical personnel, and ending with teachers and then principals. It incorporates research alongside personal experiences and anecdotes.

How do we determine the success of a school? I began this book with a predetermined set of ideas based on my experience. I thought the more money infused into education, the better the outcomes for students and schools. I was wrong. I had to expand my perspective.

Society needs to spend money on a far wider array of social needs than just education. The use of money has implications on all the factors that influence the success or failure of schools and students:

- The policies and political landscape created by federal, state, and local governments and individual school districts
- The physical plant, maintenance, and location of the school building
- Parenting
- Students, peers, and the digital age
- The roles played by nonpedagogical staff

Each factor impacts on student outcomes in critical and unique ways, and each must be considered in any method of measuring a school's success. The order above is not indicative of importance, which is determined by the uniqueness of each school and district.

The literature has addressed each of the above factors, but, as far as I can determine, no one source has looked at all these variables at the same time. When we do, we realize the lack of control teachers and school leaders have over the landscape that determines student and school success.

If we are to devise a method for evaluating the success of a school, the positive and negative impact of each factor must be included. It must be acknowledged that there are critical elements over which a school's principal or teachers have no control.

I am not going to do the impossible and present a statistical grand scheme for school evaluation. Politicians and school districts think their panoply of statistics do this. They ignore, perhaps on purpose, variables beyond the work of teachers and principals that belie the efficacy of their complex analytics.

As you read each chapter in this book, look at your own school and determine which factors have a positive or negative impact on its success. Then, look at how the school, its teachers, and its principal are rated. Have the analytics incorporated the key factors you see as important? If not, you know that the rating system is not giving a true picture of your school.

Introduction xxi

All the italicized anecdotes included are real. For the sake of anonymity, the names have been changed and locations purposely left vague.

There are two concerns you may have as you read this book.

First, you may distrust the research and statistics cited. I would if I were you! I still remember the first lecture in my first statistics class when the professor began with, "Statistics can say anything you want them to say." The internet is filled with massive amounts of data, much of it true and much amassed by fringe and advocacy groups to prove their own ideas.

I have tried to use valid and reliable sources and select the most relevant information. As you read each chapter, you will undoubtedly think of many other types of information that could have been included. So did I. Each chapter could be expanded into a book. My purpose is to provide enough information to demonstrate that each variable has a major impact on students and schools.

So you can evaluate my sources, I included the internet link (where one existed) in the bibliography. If you follow some links (as for the National Center for Education Statistics or the U.S. Census), you will find a plethora of additional information I could not include but which you might find useful and interesting. Keep in mind that websites are constantly being updated. If you check a source, you may find information and numbers updated from the time of my research.

Second, with a few notable exceptions, this book consciously avoids mention of race and ethnicity, even though, if you check the statistical sources I use, you will find considerable data regarding them. A main theme of this book is that poverty and income inequality negatively impact students and schools. These cut across racial and ethnic lines within different parts of the country, states, and even school districts.

Regardless of past history or causes, the problems of poverty and income inequality exist and are getting worse even as you read this. Schools, teachers, and principals cannot change this and operate in a society where those who can make changes are not doing so.

The book will not be as negative as it sounds. There will be suggestions on how some factors working against school and student success can be addressed and overcome.

A NOTE ON COVID-19 AND RACIAL INJUSTICE PROTESTS

The main themes of this book concern themselves with ongoing problems and issues that will not be resolved anytime soon. So, if you read this book five or more years after the publication date, it will still be relevant.

However, a few paragraphs and references will be specific to the spring and summer of 2020. My "final" draft of this book was ready to submit to Rowman & Littlefield in mid-March 2020. By then, COVID-19 was spreading unchecked. Rowman, like thousands of businesses, closed operations to protect their employees, their families, and the public.

As the shutdown continued, it became apparent I had to address the impact of this health crisis on education. As you read this book, you will notice references to COVID-19 in chapters where it seemed most appropriate. If you happen to read this book in one or two years, when, we all hope, this pandemic is controlled by an effective treatment and vaccine, these remarks will seem dated. You will also be able to judge if some of my predictions actually come to pass. Oh, for the gift of hindsight!

The protests on racial injustice began in late May 2020. This book deals with two of the most insidious underlying causes of this injustice: poverty and income inequality. Where appropriate, I make direct references to these protests. As someone who lived through the civil rights movement of the 1960s, I underwent an eerie sense of déjà vu, but with a difference. As I write this on June 11, it seems that real, systemic change and greater understanding of all the issues involved will result from today's demonstrations. Again, you will have the gift of hindsight when you read this after the 2020 elections. You will know if the justifiably angry words of the marchers became political action at the polls.

Chapter One

Money

The best parts of the annual principals' retreat were the informal discussions in the lounge after a day of workshops. A favorite topic was, what would we do if we had unlimited funds so that no child is left behind? On one particular evening, high school principal Ms. Rayne decided to make a list of what a dream school would have:

- *Laptops for every student, with new ones every five years*
- *Upgraded facilities for comfort and safety, including entrance and hallway cameras, air-conditioning, state-of the-art STEM labs, and smart boards for every classroom*
- *Reduced class sizes*
- *Full funding for the arts: teachers, band instruments, art supplies, etc.*
- *At least two full-time librarians so that the library would be available from forty minutes before the first class to one hour after the last*

The members of the informal group knew that for every child to have a chance, a school would have to go beyond instruction by providing more than the usual support services:

- *A 100:1 guidance counselor ratio; a 200:1 social worker ratio*
- *On-site medical and dental clinics*
- *On-site childcare services*
- *The ability to provide students in need with school supplies, eyeglasses, hearing aids, and even weather-appropriate clothing*

As educators, we bemoan the lack of money. If only we had more, we could do so much to help those students most in need of support. This chapter looks at how money impacts on student success. Educators think of money as funds allocated for educational spending. This is only the tip of the iceberg.

We will begin with a global perspective, comparing statistical measures of member nations of the Organisation for Economic Co-operation and Development (OECD). Then, we will look at thirty states in the United States to see how money impacts on learning. Finally, we will narrow our perspective. We will read about "a tale of two districts" on Long Island in New York State. Finally, we will home in on twenty K–5 schools in the borough of Manhattan in New York City to see what they can tell us about money and student success.

Within each of the different perspectives, we will look at one or more key questions:

- Does the amount of money spent on schools lead to significant student success?
- Do teacher salaries impact on student success?
- How do societal problems, such as poverty and income inequality, affect student and school performance?
- Can school allocations compensate for the lack of funding to address societal problems?

First, we will look at the global perspective, starting with a table of statistics mined from the OECD website. PISA is the OECD's Programme for International Assessment, a worldwide study intended to evaluate educational systems by measuring 15-year-old students' performance in literacy, mathematics literacy, and science literacy.

Usually, PISA scores are presented with the top-scoring countries first, working downward to the lowest-scoring countries. Table 1.1 goes beyond test scores, adding data on poverty, income inequality, and monetary spending. Countries are arranged according to their Childhood Poverty Ratio, moving from countries with the lowest ratio to those with the highest. Using this data, we will draw some general conclusions about the relationship of all these variables.

Table 1.1 provides a gold mine of information. We can manipulate the numbers to draw tentative conclusions. Additional information is available to readers wishing to explore other sections of the OECD website.

We must be careful when we compare and contrast countries with different cultures and populations. This is easily seen by looking at anomalies within the countries with the lowest and highest childhood poverty ratios.

Among the ten countries with the lowest childhood poverty ratios, Hungary and the Czech Republic, for example, have below-average student achieve-

Table 1.1. Poverty, Spending, and Student Achievement among OECD Member Nations

	1	2	3	4	5	6	7	8	9
Country	Childhood Poverty Ratio	Inequality Level Rank	% of GDP for Education	Early Childhood Spending per Child	Primary Spending per Child	Secondary Spending per Child	PISA 2018 Literacy Average: 487	PISA 2018 Math Literacy Average: 489	PISA 2018 Science Literacy Average: 489
Ten Countries with the Lowest Childhood Poverty Ratios									
Finland	0.036	8	3.970	12,300	9,300	10,500	520	507	522
Denmark	0.037	5	4.674	11,500	12,200	13,400	501	509	493
Iceland	0.058	4	4.376	13,900	11,200	11,100	474	495	475
Slovenia	0.071	2	2.955	8,600	8,500	8,300	495	509	507
Hungary	0.077	9	2.674	6,800	5,100	5,900	476	481	481
Norway	0.080	6	4.612	17,200	13,200	15,400	499	501	490
Czech Rep	0.085	3	2.424	5,000	5,200	8,500	490	499	497
Poland	0.093	12	2.929	6,200	6,800	6,800	512	516	511
Sweden	0.093	10	3.646	14,900	10,900	11,400	506	502	499
Estonia	0.096	19	2.749	6,500	6,300	6,900	523	523	530
Lowest 10 Poverty Ratio Averages	*0.076*	*7.8*	*3.501*	*10,290*	*8,870*	*8,295*	*499.6*	*504.2*	*500.5*
The Fifteen Countries "in the Middle"									
Ireland	0.100	17	2.511	6,100	8,300	10,100	518	500	496
Netherlands	0.109	13	3.176	8,400	8,500	12,800	485	519	503
Austria	0.115	11	2.978	9,800	11,700	15,500	484	499	490
France	0.115	14	3.398	7,900	7,400	11,700	493	495	493
Canada	0.116	18	3.169	NA	9,200	NA	520	512	518
Belgium	0.123	7	4.130	NA	10,200	13,300	493	508	499
Germany	0.123	15	2.608	11,100	8,600	11,800	498	500	503
Australia	0.125	21	3.182	7,100	9,500	13,200	503	491	503
United Kingdom	0.129	30	3.783	9,000	11,600	10,600	504	502	505
Luxembourg	0.130	16	2.794	20,500	20,900	20,400	470	483	477
Latvia	0.132	27	3.254	5,300	6,700	6,900	479	496	487
Japan	0.139	24	2.479	7,500	9,100	11,100	504	521	529
Slovak Rep	0.140	1	2.554	5,900	6,900	6,700	458	486	464
New Zealand	0.141	28	3.784	13,500	7,920	10,400	506	494	508
Korea	0.145	29	3.469	NA	11,000	12,200	514	526	519

(continued)

Table 1.1. Continued

	1	2	3	4	5	6	7	8	9
Country	Childhood Poverty Ratio	Inequality Level Rank	% of GDP for Education	Early Childhood Spending per Child	Primary Spending per Child	Secondary Spending per Child	PISA 2018 Literacy Average: 487	PISA 2018 Math Literacy Average: 489	PISA 2018 Science Literacy Average: 489
Ten Countries with the Highest Childhood Poverty Ratios									
Portugal	0.155	22	3.392	7,100	7,400	9,500	492	492	492
Italy	0.173	20	2.780	6,200	8,400	9,100	476	487	468
Greece	0.176	23	2.660	NA	5,800	6,800	457	451	452
Lithuania	0.177	31	2.315	5,500	5,500	5,200	476	481	482
Mexico	0.198	34	3.204	2,700	2,900	3,100	420	409	419
United States	0.212	32	3.207	10,000*	11,700	13,100	505	478	502
Chile	0.215	35	3.026	6,100	5,100	4,900	452	417	444
Spain	0.220	25	2.656	7,000	7,300	9,000	NA	481	483
Israel	0.237	26	4.033	4,200	8,000	NA	470	463	462
Turkey	0.253	33	2.533	3,600	4,100	3,500	466	454	468
Highest 10 Poverty Ratio Averages	*0.202*	*28.1*	*2.981*	*5,822*	*5,450*	*7,133*	*468.2*	*461.3*	*467.2*

Sources

Column 1: Organisation for Economic Co-operation and Development. n.d.d. "Poverty Rate." https://data.oecd.org/inequality/poverty-rate.htm#indicator-chart.
Column 2: Organisation for Economic Co-operation and Development. n.d.a. "Income Inequality: OECD Data." https://data.oecd.org/inequality/income-inequality.htm.
Columns 3, 4, 5, and 6: Organisation for Economic Co-operation and Development. n.d.b. "Percent of Gross Domestic Product and Monetary Expense in US Dollars for Primary to Post-Secondary, Non-tertiary: OECD Data." https://data.oecd.org/eduresource/public-spending-on-education.htm.
Column 4: Source for Information on Early Childhood Spending in the US: Camera, Lauren. 2017. "U.S. Trails in Early Childhood Education Enrollment." *U.S. News and World Report*, June 21, 2017. https://www.usnews.com/news/best-countries/articles/2017-06-21/us-falls-behind-other-developed-countries-in-early-childhood-education-enrollment.
Columns 7, 8, and 9: Organisation for Economic Co-operation and Development. n.d.c. "PISA 2018." http://www.oecd.org/pisa/.

Notes

1. Only OECD member nations are included in this chart. Member nations Argentina and Columbia have been excluded because data on poverty and income inequality is not available. Switzerland has been excluded because data on educational spending is unavailable.
2. As per the OECD, the poverty rate (Column 1) is the ratio of the number of people (in a given age group) whose income falls below the poverty line, taken as half the median household income of the total population.
3. The OECD uses a complicated ratio to determine income inequality. Column 2 makes use of these ratios to rank the thirty-five nations on the chart, with #1 having the lowest income inequality and #35 having the highest income inequality.
4. Columns 4, 5, and 6 are expressed in US dollars, rounded to the nearest 100.

ment as measured by PISA scores. This could be related to the relatively low amount of public spending on education at all levels. Estonia, on the other hand, spends below average on education but has stellar PISA scores.

Looking at the ten countries with the highest childhood poverty ratios, we find the United States with relatively high education spending and PISA scores (except in mathematics literacy, where the U.S. ranks thirtieth out of the thirty-five countries examined).

When we stop looking at the exceptions and compare the *average* statistics for the ten countries with the lowest childhood poverty ratios with the ten counties with the highest childhood poverty ratios, we find that countries in the former group:

- Have a lower average income inequality rank, 7.9 compared to 29.1 (column 2)
- Spend a significantly higher percentage of their gross domestic products on education, 3.501 compared to 2.981 (column 3)
- Spend more public funds on education, particularly for early childhood education, $10,290 compared to $5,822 (column 4)
- Have significantly higher average PISA scores: +31 in literacy (column 7), +43 in mathematics literacy (column 8), and +33 in science literacy (column 9)

What accounts for the difference in the PISA scores—education spending or the countries' low childhood poverty ratio and low-income inequality rank? It is very tempting to just look at the dollar amounts and say it is due to education spending. But countries with high poverty have fewer resources to devote to education. Five of the countries with high childhood poverty ratios—Portugal, Mexico, the United States, Chile, and Israel—spend an average of 3.37 of their GDP on education. But, except for the United States, the actual dollar amounts pale in comparison to most of the countries with the lowest poverty ratios.

Let's add some information about the twenty countries we are looking at: What are their national policies regarding paid maternity/paternity leave?

Children spend far more time at home with parents and family than they do in school, as we will explore further in Chapter 4.

The ten countries with the lowest childhood poverty levels, on average, provide nearly double the paid maternity/paternity leave as countries with the highest childhood poverty levels. Low childhood poverty countries seem to put high value on the role of parents during the most formative year of a child's life. Could this factor lead to higher achievement in school? Could

Table 1.2. Maternity/Paternity Leave: Selected OECD Countries

	Ten OECD Countries with the Lowest Poverty Ratios		
Country	Column 1 Maternity/Paternity Leave Length	Column 2 Percentage of Wages Paid	Column 3 Days
Finland	105 days of maternity leave	70%	105
Denmark	52 weeks of maternity leave	100%	365
Iceland	3 months of maternity; 3 months of paternity; 3 additional months that can be taken by either parent	80%	270
Slovenia	105 days of maternity leave	100%	105
Hungary	24 weeks of maternity leave	70%	168
Norway	36 to 46 weeks of parental leave	Benefits are paid at 100% for the shorter duration and 80% for the longer option.	322
Czech Rep	28 weeks of maternity leave	60%	198
Poland	20 weeks of maternity leave	100%	140
Sweden	420 days	80%	420
Estonia	140 days of maternity leave	100%	140
Average number of paid (at least 50% of salary) maternity/paternity days			223

	Ten OECD Countries with the Highest Poverty Ratios		
Country	Column 1 Maternity/Paternity Leave Length	Column 2 Percentage of Wages Paid	Column 3 Days
Portugal	120 to 150 days of parental leave	Benefits are paid at 100% for the shorter duration and 80% for the longer option.	150
Italy	5 months of maternity leave	80%; there is an additional option for six months leave at 30%	150
Greece	119 days of maternity leave	50%	119
Lithuania	126 days of maternity leave	100%	126
Mexico (1)	6 weeks of maternity leave	100%; can be extended 6 more weeks at 50%	84
United States	14 weeks of maternity leave	No federal policy for any payments	0
Chile (2)	18 weeks	Government subsidy; can choose 12 additional weeks at 50% of the subsidy (may not be 50% or more of salary)	210

Country	Column 1 Maternity/Paternity Leave Length	Column 2 Percentage of Wages Paid	Column 3 Days
	Ten OECD Countries with the Highest Poverty Ratios		
Spain	16 weeks of maternity leave	100%	112
Israel (3)	105 days	100%	105
Turkey (4)	16 weeks	100%	112
Average number of paid (at least 50% of salary) maternity/paternity days			117

Sources

Huffington Post Canada. 2012. "Maternity Leaves Around the World: Worst and Best Countries for Paid Maternity Leave." Updated November 18, 2015. https://www.huffingtonpost.ca/2012/05/22/maternity-leaves-around-the-world_n_1536120.html.
AngloInfo. N.d. "Find Out about the Leaves and Benefit Entitlements for Parents in Mexico." https://www.angloinfo.com/how-to/mexico/healthcare/pregnancy-birth/maternity-rights.
"Working in Chile: Maternity Leave." 2015. *Inside Santiago: Expat Living Blog*, May 12, 2015. https://insidesantiago.wordpress.com/category/working-in-chile-job-finding-tips/.
National Insurance Institute of Israel. n.d. "Maternity Allowance: Period of Entitlement." https://www.btl.gov.il/English%20Homepage/Benefits/Maternity%20Insurance/Maternity%20Allowance/Pages/Maximum.aspx.
Turkish Labor Law. 2016. "Maternity Leave in Turkey." https://turkishlaborlaw.com/news/business-in-turkey/423-maternity-leave-in-turkey.

Notes on Column 3

1. The number of days listed is the maximum allowed with at least 50% of salary paid. Countries define "week" and "month" differently (some include weekends, some do not). For the purposes of this column, a week will be seven days and a month thirty days.
2. The government subsidy in Chile is a set sum not related to the salary earned. The website on Turkey does not say what paid maternity leave means in terms of money. For the purposes of this column, both were given the benefit of the doubt, and it was assumed that both paid at least 50% of the employee's salary.

this mean that early parental training will lead to better socialization skills and fewer negative behaviors in later life? What do the numbers say about the United States with no national paid parental leave policy?

We began with a global perspective. Given the many variables outside those explored in the two tables, it is difficult to draw precise conclusions. The size of a country, for example, is important. Estonia has a total population of 1.3 million; this is only slightly higher than the student population of the New York City public school system. The percentage of a country's population speaking the same language and each country's immigration rate also impact on PISA scores. There are also the variables of teacher recruitment, training, and pay as well as the relative prestige of the teaching profession in different nations.

For now, let's just conclude that dollar spending on K–12 education may not be the most important factor leading to student achievement. Childhood poverty, income inequality, national policies on parental leave, and spending on early childhood education all enter into the equation.

As we home in on the United States, let's keep in mind how it ranks with much of the rest of the world: extremely high childhood poverty ratio and

8   *Chapter One*

income inequality rank; fourteenth out of thirty-five nations in percentage of GDP spent on education; no national policy on paid parental leave. Within the thirty-five OECD nations in the table, the US PISA score for literacy ranks ninth; for mathematics literacy, thirtieth; for science literacy, thirteenth.

There is a mountain of statistical information on the United States. Multiple sources were consulted to create a table that combines information on those states spending the most and the least on education. Take a few minutes to look at Table 1.3 to absorb the information it contains.

To fully understand the data presented, we need to understand the meaning of the regional price parity index (Column 3). This number is used to equalize the buying power of dollar amounts so that arguments about the divergent costs of living in different states can be eliminated.

Column 5 adjusts the total dollars spent per pupil using this index. As you can clearly see, states with higher costs of living actually spend less per pupil than the dollar amount because the dollar in these states has less purchasing power; likewise, states with lower costs of living actually spend more per pupil because the purchasing power of a dollar is greater.

Column 6 gives the adjusted average teaching salary, using the regional price parity index. The index in New York State is 115.3. In New York, the actual average teacher salary (2016–2017) was $79,637. However, when you divide this by the index, you find that the actual buying power of this salary in New York was $69,069. In Alabama, the index is 86.8. The average teacher's salary (2016–2017) of $48,686 has an actual buying power of $56,090. So, on paper, it looks like a teacher in New York earns $30,951 more than a teacher in Alabama ($79,637–$48,686) but in terms of actual buying power, the New York teacher earns $12,979 more than the teacher in Alabama.

Table 1.3 includes over half of the country, clumping together the fifteen states spending the most money per pupil and the fifteen states spending the least money per pupil. While the following conclusions may not be applicable to an individual state in each group, they are to the group as a whole. In this way anomalies are subsumed by the whole. What do we learn from the information in Table 1.3?

- Even when a price parity index is applied (Column 5), there is a wide disparity of spending on education. In adjusted dollars, the highest spending states devote an average of nearly $6,000 more per pupil per year than the lowest spending states.
- This is most clearly seen in the price parity index adjusted teacher salaries (Column 6). The highest spending states have an adjusted average teacher salary over $10,700 higher that the lowest spending states. That's a 20.7% difference.

Table 1.3. States Spending the Most and the Least on Education per Pupil

1	2	3	4	5	6	7	8	9
Rank in $ Spent	State	Regional Price Parity Index	Total per Pupil	Adjusted Total per Pupil	Adjusted Average Teacher Salary 2016–2017	% of Students Eligible for Free Lunch 2015–2016	Education Week: K–12 Student Achievement Score 2018	% Below Poverty Level
Fifteen States Spending the Most per Pupil								
1	New York	115.3	22,366	19,398	69,069	49.5	72.8	14.1
2	District of Columbia	117.0	19,159	16,375	65,069	76.4	66.5	16.6
3	Connecticut	108.7	18,958	17,441	66,753	37.9	74.6	9.6
4	New Jersey	113.4	18,402	16,228	61,396	37.6	84.7	10.0
5	Vermont	101.6	17,873	17,592	59,239	38.4	73.0	11.3
6	Alaska	105.6	17,510	16,581	64,525	42.7	62.8	11.1
7	Wyoming	96.2	16,442	17,091	60,967	37.5	73.1	11.3
8	Massachusetts	106.9	15,593	14,687	72,782	39.9	88.0	10.5
9	Rhode Island	98.7	15,532	15,737	67,352	47.0	70.5	11.6
10	Pennsylvania	97.9	15,418	15,749	67,276	48.2	76.0	12.5
11	New Hampshire	105.0	15,340	14,610	54,527	28.3	77.2	7.7
12	Delaware	100.4	14,713	14,654	59,974	37.7	68.8	13.6
13	Maryland	109.6	14,206	12,962	61,096	45.0	77.7	9.3
14	Illinois	99.7	14,180	14,223	61,787	49.6	73.3	12.6
15	Hawaii	118.8	13,744	11,569	48,876	49.9	71.0	9.5
AVERAGES			16,629	15,660	62,713	44.37	74.0	11.42
Fifteen States Spending the Least per Pupil								
1	Utah	97.0	6,953	7,168	48,705	36.4	73.9	9.7
2	Idaho	93.4	7,157	7,663	50,861	46.9	72.0	12.8
3	Arizona	96.2	7,613	7,914	49,275	50.2	71.6	14.9
4	Oklahoma	89.9	8,097	9,016	50,328	62.2	64.0	15.8

(continued)

Table 1.3. Continued

1	2	3	4	5	6	7	8	9
Rank in $ Spent	State	Regional Price Parity Index	Total per Pupil	Adjusted Total per Pupil	Adjusted Average Teacher Salary 2016–2017	% of Students Eligible for Free Lunch 2015–2016	Education Week: K-12 Student Achievement Score 2018	% Below Poverty Level
5	Mississippi	86.2	8,702	10,095	49,797	74.9	64.1	19.8
6	North Carolina	91.2	8,792	9,640	54,646	57.4	72.0	14.7
7	Tennessee	89.0	8,810	9,899	54,445	58.8	70.8	15.0
8	Florida	99.5	8,920	8,965	49,655	58.8	78.4	14.0
9	Nevada	98.0	8,960	9,143	58,547	58.8	67.3	13.0
10	Texas	96.8	9,016	9,314	54,313	58.9	70.6	14.7
11	South Dakota	88.2	9,176	10,404	48,376	41.7	68.8	13.0
12	Alabama	86.8	9,236	10,641	56,090	51.1	66.1	16.9
13	Colorado	103.2	9,575	9,278	45,064	41.8	73.8	10.3
14	New Mexico	94.4	9,693	10,268	50,318	71.7	61.5	19.7
15	Georgia	92.6	9,769	10,550	58,965	62.4	74.7	14.9
AVERAGES			8,698	9,331	51,960	55.46	70.0	12.76

Sources

Columns 1 and 4: Governing.com. 2016. "Education Spending Per Student by State." Updated June 1, 2018. https://www.governing.com/gov-data/education-data/state-education-spending-per-pupil-data.html. Rankings derived from the dollar amounts provided in column 4.
Column 3: Mulhere, Kaitlin. 2018. "This Map Shows the Average Cost of Living in Every State and What It's Worth." Money. Updated March 15, 2018. https://money.com/average-income-every-state-real-value/. This article uses a regional price parity index to allow for the comparison of the buying power within the states.
Column 5: Column 4 divided by column 3. The amounts in this column have been adjusted by the regional price parity index so that the salaries in each state can be more equitably compared.
Column 6: National Center for Education Statistics. n.d.c. "Table 211.60 Estimated Average Annual Salary of Teachers in Public Elementary and Secondary Schools, by State: Selected Years, 1969-70 through 2016-17." https://nces.ed.gov/programs/digest/d17/tables/dt17_211.60.asp. The 2016–2017 salaries provided have been divided by the regional price parity index from the third column to give the "adjusted" dollar amounts, allowing salaries to be better compared.
Column 7: National Center for Education Statistics. n.d.b. "Table 204.10 Number and Percentage of Public School Students Eligible for Free or Reduced-Price Lunch by State: Selected Years 2000-01 through 2015-16." https://nces.ed.gov/programs/digest/d16/tables/dt16_204.10.asp.
Column 8: "Quality Counts 2018: Report and Rankings: A Report Card for States and the Nation on K-12 Education." 2019. Education Week. Published June 20, 2018. https://www.edweek.org/ew/collections/quality-counts-2018-state-grades/index.html. The website describes the method of determining the rankings.
Column 9: U.S. Census Bureau. n.d. "Percentage of People in Poverty by State Using 2- and 3-Year Averages: 2015–2016 and 2017–2018." https://www.census.gov/data/tables/2019/demo/income-poverty/p60-266.html.

- Using the *Education Week* ratings for student success, students in the higher spending states have about a 4% higher achievement rate than those in the lower spending states, 74% to 70%.

Let's look at another possible factor impacting on achievement. In Table 1.4, the states have been reordered, grouping the fifteen states with the highest poverty levels and the fifteen states with the lowest poverty levels. This is matched with data on student achievement and free/reduced lunch eligibility.

What does Table 1.4 tell us? Students in low poverty states score 6.2% higher than their counterparts in high poverty states.

Table 1.3 indicates that a state's spending on education led to a 4% higher achievement rate. Table 1.4 indicates that states with lower poverty see a 6.2% higher achievement rate. It would seem that poverty level has greater impact on student achievement than spending on education. This tentative conclusion is supported when we look at five of the six states that are anomalies.

We would expect that states spending the most on education would have the least poverty and states spending the least on education would have the most poverty. Not true. Utah, Colorado, and Idaho are low education spending states with low poverty levels All three have relatively high student achievement scores. Alaska and the District of Columbia have high education spending and high poverty levels. Their student achievement scores are relatively low. New York alone has high spending, high poverty and a relatively high student achievement score.

Within the United States, statistical explanations are complicated. A state is a conglomerate of districts. Each district may have higher or lower property tax dollars to add to the federal and state education budget. Different states have different formulas for the support they provide local schools, with many trying to compensate for property tax support inequalities.

The same factors that impact on entire countries affect individual states regarding student achievement: size, common cultural norms, native English speakers, and immigration. You can also add to this mix the number of urban vs. suburban vs. rural residents.

Looking at groupings of states establishes a relationship between poverty and educational outcomes, but we need to look further. We need to move down to the district level.

The relationship between poverty and achievement becomes far clearer when we look at Tables 1.5, 1.6, and 1.7, which compare data pertaining to two Long Island school districts. These districts are separated by only twelve miles but are a universe apart in terms of poverty, income inequality, and student achievement.

Table 1.4. Poverty Level and Student Achievement

Fifteen States with the Highest Poverty Levels

#	State	Education Week: K–12 Student Achievement Score 2018	% Below Poverty Level 2016–2018	% of Students Eligible for Free Lunch 2015–2016
1	Mississippi	64.1	19.8	74.9
2	New Mexico	61.5	18.7	71.7
3	Alabama	66.1	16.0	51.1
4	District of Columbia	66.5	14.9	76.4
5	Georgia	74.7	14.7	62.4
6	Arizona	71.6	14.4	50.2
7	North Carolina	72.0	14.1	57.4
8	Oklahoma	64.0	14.0	62.2
9	Texas	70.6	13.7	58.9
10	Florida	78.4	13.6	58.8
11	Tennessee	70.8	12.6	58.8
12	Nevada	67.3	12.2	58.8
13	Alaska	62.8	12.2	42.7
14	South Dakota	68.8	11.8	41.7
15	New York	72.8	11.8	49.5
	AVERAGES	68.93	14.3	58.37

Fifteen States with the Lowest Poverty Levels

#	State	Education Week: K–12 Student Achievement Score 2018	% Below Poverty Level 2016–2018	% of Students Eligible for Free Lunch 2015–2016
1	New Hampshire	77.2	6.4	28.3
2	Maryland	77.7	7.1	45.0
3	Utah	73.9	7.9	36.4
4	Colorado	73.8	8.9	41.8
5	New Jersey	84.7	9.1	37.6
6	Hawaii	71.0	9.5	49.9
7	Vermont	73.0	9.6	38.4
8	Delaware	68.8	9.6	37.7
9	Massachusetts	88.0	9.8	39.9
10	Connecticut	74.6	9.9	37.9
11	Rhode Island	70.5	10.3	47.0
12	Illinois	73.3	10.9	49.6
13	Idaho	72.0	11.3	46.9
14	Pennsylvania	76.0	11.5	48.2
15	Wyoming	73.1	11.4	37.5
	AVERAGES	75.17	9.55	41.47

Table 1.5. Economic/Income Inequality

		Syosset Central School District	Wyandanch Union Free School District
1	Income per Capita	$61,099	$17,922
2	Income per Household	$133,110	$54,616
3	Income below Poverty Line	2.5%	15.5%
4	Homeownership Rate	92.7%	59.2%
5	Home Median Value	$648,200	$284,400
6	Need Rank	656/674	2/674
7	Wealth Decile (with 10 being the most wealthy and 1 the least)	10/10	1/10

Sources

Rows 1–5: "Wyandanch Union Free School District, New York Demographics." 2020. *biggestcities.com*. Updated January 17, 2020. https://www.biggestuscities.com/demographics/ny/wyandanch-union-free-school-district.

Rows 6–7: Citizens Budget Commission. 2017. "New York per Pupil Education Spending Is Nation's Highest: Where Does the Money Come From?" Published September 7, 2017. https://cbcny.org/research/new-york-pupil-education-spending-nations-highest. Note: The CBC gives each school district in the state a ranking from 1 (the lowest need) to 674 (the highest need).

Table 1.5 makes it clear that income inequality exists between these two districts, with one in the top wealth decile and the other at the bottom.

There are several ways to look at the data in Table 1.6. Do higher teacher salaries lead to higher student achievement? Or are the salaries on a par with

Table 1.6. Per Pupil Spending, Teacher Salaries, Teacher Turnover, and Class Sizes

		Syosset Central School District	Wyandanch Union Free School District
1	Per Pupil Spending	$33,676	$24,296
2	Turnover Rate of Teachers with Less than 5 Years of Experience	16%	0%
3	Turnover Rate of All Teachers	6%	11%
4	Class Size Range	19–25	21–27
	Contractual Teacher Salary Scales		
5	Master's Degree 2018–2019	72,400 to 131,618 (26 steps)	57,911 to 104,914 (20 steps)
6	Master's Degree + 30 credits 2018–2019	78,937 to 138,084 (26 steps)	62,830 to 107,405 (20 steps)
7	Master's Degree + 60 credits 2018–2019	85,478 to 144,566 (26 steps)	67,194 to 114,374 (20 steps)

Sources

Lines 1–4: New York State Education Department. n.d. "Wyandanch UFSD at a Glance." https://data.nysed.gov/profile.php?instid=800000037741; New York State Education Department. n.d. "Syosset CSD at a Glance." https://data.nysed.gov/profile.php?instid=800000048948.

Lines 5–7: Agreement between the Syosset Central School District, County of Nassau, Syosset, New York and the Syosset Teachers Association, July 1, 2017–June 30, 2020. https://www.syossetschools.org/site/handlers/filedownload.ashx?moduleinstanceid=832&dataid=9296&FileName=Syosset_Teachers_Assoc.pdf; Agreement between Board of Education Wyandanch Union Free School District and Wyandanch Teachers' Association, July 1, 2016–June 30, 2022.

the cost of living and housing in the district? Does a high teacher turnover rate during the first five years (line 2) indicate that Syosset has many applicants and can therefore discontinue less than able teachers? Or is the district making sure that fewer teachers reach the higher salary levels by not renewing contracts and hiring teachers at the entry level?

New York State has tried to equalize the playing field. While the amount spent per pupil is higher in Syosset, state aid has made the amount spent per pupil in Wyandanch a hefty $24,296. How was this done? The Wyandanch Proposed 2019–2020 Budget indicates that nearly 58% of its proposed expenditures will come from state aid, while only 28% will come from tax levy sources (primarily property taxes). According to the Syosset CSD Report Card, 2018–2019 Proposed Budget, state aid accounts for 7% of the budget while tax levies account for 85%.

Despite this, it is clear from Table 1.7 that there is a vast student achievement gap between these two districts. State educational support for the Wyandanch district cannot overcome the negative effects of poverty, leading to a poorer student achievement and a much lower graduation rate.

We can home in even closer by looking at part of one district in a large urban setting. New York City, with more than one million students, is considered

Table 1.7. Student Characteristics and Achievement Statistics 2017–2018

		Syosset Central School District	Wyandanch Union Free School District
1	Economically Disadvantaged Students	9%	95%
2	Students with Disabilities	11%	18%
3	English Language Learners	3%	31%
4	ELA Proficient (Aggregate)	77%	22%
5	Math Proficient (Aggregate)	88%	14%
6	Graduation Rate	98%	66%
7	Graduation with a Regents Diploma	97%	60%
8	Graduation with an Advanced Regents Diploma	84%	5%

Source

New York State Education Department. n.d. "Wyandanch UFSD at a Glance." https://data.nysed.gov/profile.php?instid=800000037741; New York State Education Department. n.d. "Syosset CSD at a Glance." https://data.nysed.gov/profile.php?instid=800000048948.

New York is one of the few states requiring students to pass state-prepared tests (the Regents examinations) to earn a high school diploma.

—To earn a Regents diploma, a student must pass one exam each in ELA, mathematics, science, and social studies; they must also demonstrate competency on a state-approved assessment in one of several pathways: CTE, CDOS, the arts, the humanities, or STEM.

—To earn an Advanced Regents diploma, the student must complete all of the above plus two additional math courses and one additional science course.

For complete information, go to http://www.nysed.gov/curriculum-instruction/diploma-types.

one district. We are going to examine a small slice of this district by looking at ten "high" and ten "low" rated schools in the borough of Manhattan.

Savvy parents check district websites for data on student achievement. They also go to websites like greatschools.org to look for independent ratings of schools; this website was consulted for the selection of schools listed in Table 1.8.

Parents use the information they find to select schools for their children, even if it means moving into the appropriate school district. Highly rated schools are considered "destination schools," that is, schools that are so good, parents will relocate just so their children can be assigned to them. In this era of school choice, more and more parents are using school statistics to determine school preferences for their children.

The information in Table 1.8 is culled from the School Quality Guide 2017–2018 found at the Department of Education NYC website, https://tools.nycenet.edu/snapshot/2018/.

This comparison within one district helps eliminate variables. All teachers meet the same certification requirements and are on the same salary scale. All schools are funded according to the same formula, though high need schools that qualify for Title I and other federal grants receive extra monies.

Within 22.75 square miles of Manhattan, there can be huge differences in the poverty levels of adjoining neighborhoods and even between the poverty level of students attending schools across the street from one another.

What conclusions can we draw from Table 1.8?

- The poverty level of students and their families in the schools with the higher student achievement ratings is significantly lower than the poverty level in the schools with the lower student achievement ratings. "Disparity" is too kind a word—there is a chasm of inequality with the Economic Need Index of the lower achieving schools over four times greater than that of the higher achieving schools.
- The schools with the higher Economic Need Indexes have significantly poorer student achievement ratings.
- There are anomalies. Schools 110 and 130 have good student achievement ratings despite relatively high economic need. School 200, with an extremely high Economic Need Index has relatively high student achievement. Is this caused by variables in proximate neighborhoods, or, by some chance, did the perfect combination of school leaders and teachers coalesce to help students reach a higher level of achievement?

There is also a disparity in the percentage of the student populations classified as students with disabilities and as ELLs. Recent research has shown

Table 1.8. Comparison of High- and Low-Achieving NYC K–5 Elementary Schools in Manhattan

	High-Achieving Schools				Low-Achieving Schools		
School	Economic Need Index	Percentage of Students with Disabilities or ELL	Student Achievement Rating	School	Economic Need Index	Percentage of Students with Disabilities or ELL	Student Achievement Rating
77	10.1	10.1	4.82	194	96.9	48.6	2.86
6	11.2	21.5	4.38	155	96.8	77.0	2.65
40	14.4	21.4	4.31	200	94.4	46.5	3.87
41	8.0	17.7	4.30	197	92.5	41.5	2.62
110	59.4	17.2	4.23	133	90.1	45.9	2.56
130	58.6	30.9	4.45	132	90.5	75.7	3.43
183	7.1	21.9	4.14	98	89.5	60.4	2.91
89	9.2	21.4	4.31	38	93.7	53.0	2.48
234	9.5	18.4	4.27	189	88.9	60.0	3.29
452	28.2	25.2	4.44	129	93.5	36.6	3.34
AVER	21.57	20.57	4.365	AVER	92.68	54.52	3.001

Note

The economic need index is a percentage that incorporates the percentage of students eligible for HRA assistance, the percentage of families below the federal poverty level (estimated), and the percentage of students in temporary housing. Student achievement ratings, ranging from 1 to 5, are based on New York State Metrics, which incorporates average student ELA performance (15%), average student ELA performance of the lowest one-third (15%), average student math performance (15%), average student math performance of the lowest one-third (15%), percentage of students at ELA levels 3 and 4 (15%), percentage of math students at levels 3 and 4 (15%), and 10% for "next level readiness."

that the day-to-day trauma of poverty can cause children to exhibit traits that have them inaccurately labeled as "students with disabilities" (see Chapter 5). And, of course, students whose native language is not English need additional supports.

This chapter has taken the form of a funnel. It moves from a world view, to a country view, to a district view, and finally to schools within a district. As we move from top to bottom, the impact of poverty and income inequality on student achievement becomes increasingly apparent.

What does this data mean to the school leaders and teachers of our nation? It tells them that the impact they have on the lives of children is limited by the egregious income inequality and dire poverty of children and families in a nation that is, ironically, an economic powerhouse.

As the opening of this chapter illustrates, every competent principal knows that more money is needed not only for school-related instruction and curriculum but also for the basic needs of students through counseling, medical care, and even food and clothing. But the money is not there.

In one of the richest nations in the world, millions live in poverty—and their living standards continue to deteriorate. The gap between the rich and poor is widening. The middle class is shrinking. Wealth is concentrated in the top 1% of the population.

Principals and other educators can join protest movements to fight for social programs and policies to lessen income inequality. Such protests have yielded meager results in the past and take time and effort away from their main job: the education of children.

They can also lobby federal, state, and local authorities for more educational spending and better school budgets. But increased school budgets, while helpful, have no effect on the poverty of families and children.

Educators can apply for grants from nonprofits, but monies received would be a small enhancement of the inadequate school allocation. Often, the staff time and effort devoted to implementing and assessing such grants can nullify some of its effects.

The bottom line is simple: money to combat poverty and income inequality and money to provide for better schools and instruction are critical factors in the success of children and schools, critical factors over which principals and teachers have very little control.

The Economic Need Index included in Table 1.8 is found on the NYC Department of Education website, telling us that the statisticians know about this factor and know that poverty levels impact on student and school success. But is it given the weight it should have in their complicated analytics rating teachers and school leaders?

Chapter Two

"The Powers That Be"

In Chapter 1 we discovered that money allocated to schools had limited impact on student achievement. More efficacious was money allocated for social programs to reduce poverty and income inequality.

Though limited in efficacy, money for schools is important. We will begin this chapter looking at how allocations are made and then examine how federal, state, local, and district policies and the political landscape as a whole impact schools.

Schools have three basic funding sources: local (sometimes, called tax levy because it derives from taxation, often property taxes), state, and federal. Private grants are available for specific programs, but these are insignificant compared to the other sources.

School leaders and teachers have little control over the budgets their schools receive. They can make sure that a high percentage of parents complete lunch applications to improve their chances of receiving Title I funding, which can add up to 10% of a school's budget. They can apply for other federal grants for which the school may be eligible. They can look to private grant sources as the well-known Gates Foundation. But nearly 90% of the budget is a given.

Parents have been known to organize and protest for more funds. Teachers have been known to go on strike. Principals make special appeals to superintendents. Their impact is negligible.

Tax levy funding is zip code determined. As we saw in "a tale of two districts" in Chapter 1, the wealthier the community, the more money generated. State funding attempts to make up for tax levy disparities, but there is never enough money to do this completely.

Officially, Title I federal funding goes to schools in School Wide or Targeted School Assistance programs. Schools with a student base where at least

40% come from low-income families qualify for the School Wide Program, which allows schools to merge all funding sources to upgrade the school's programs. Schools under this threshold of 40% receive supplemental funds to provide services only to selected students with the greatest need of assistance, usually through distinctly funded teachers, paraprofessionals, and counselors.

This is not always the case. Funds are funneled through school districts. Sometimes, the funding is insufficient for the needs of the students in the district. In some large urban areas, a school must meet a threshold of 60% to be eligible for School Wide programs (i.e., 60% of the students must qualify for free or reduced lunch). Federal funds are limited; the needs of students are not. The more schools eligible for Title I funds, the fewer the dollars allocated to each school.

Higher allocations may improve student achievement but cannot compensate for the poverty and income inequality of the United States as a whole or within each individual district. Whatever their impact, budget allocations are outside the purview of school leaders and teachers.

A new type of crisis in school funding looms for the 2020–2021 school year "in the wake of school closures amid the Covid-19 pandemic. In April alone, 469,000 public school district personnel nationally lost their jobs, including kindergarten through twelfth-grade teachers and other school employees, a Labor Department economist told Reuters" (Paltrow 2020). Paltrow adds that such personnel loss could last for four years, impacting all students but particularly those in poorer school districts. "Poorer districts, where property tax revenue is low, rely on states for most of their income. With states hit hard by falling income and sales taxes, aid to school districts is dwindling in many places."

Billions in federal support is needed to prevent these and other teacher layoffs. Only time will tell if a divided Congress will pass such a bailout bill.

National policies, also outside the purview of teachers and school leaders, impact on education. Some of these are obvious, and some are not. Let's begin with the most obvious.

Twenty years ago, in an article for the *New York Times Magazine*, "What No School Can Do," Frank Traub wrote:

> The idea that school, by itself, cannot cure poverty is hardly astonishing, but it is amazing how much of our political discourse is implicitly predicated on the notion that it can. . . . It is hard to think of a more satisfying solution to poverty than education. School reform involves relatively little money and no large-scale initiatives, asks practically nothing of the nonpoor and is accompanied by the ennobling sensation that comes from expressing faith in the capacity of the poor to overcome disadvantage by themselves (Traub 2000, 56).

Nothing has changed. The policies of the federal government seem to postulate that schools alone can fix the problems of society and do so with less money.

The proposed 2018 federal budget allocated 3% to education, 9% to welfare (housing, workers' compensation, food stamps, unemployment, and welfare payments), 28% to health care, and 21% to defense. In terms of dollars allocated, the proposed 2018 budget represented the following changes (Soffen and Lu 2017; Parlapiano and Aisch 2017):

- 9% increase for the Department of Defense
- 7% increase for the Department of Homeland Security
- 21% decrease for the Department of Agriculture (including the elimination of food for education)
- 18% decrease for the Department of Health and Human Services
- 13% decrease for the Department of Housing and Urban Development
- 14% decrease for the Department of Education (cutting grants and programs for teacher training, after-school and summer care, and aid to low-income students)
- 5% decrease in the Small Business Administration

Allocations for areas providing human services to reduce poverty are being slashed along with funding for educational support. This is a long way from LBJ's Great Society and indicative of current federal priorities, which do not include education or social welfare. More citizens will suffer the pangs of poverty, and the gap between rich and poor will continue to widen.

Implementation of the Common Core Standards caused problems for elementary school principal Ms. Wren. The parents complained that the standards (especially in mathematics) were incomprehensible. The matter was complicated by her district, which issued standardized lesson plans for the teachers, causing them to bitterly complain about the lack of trust in their abilities and experience and the loss of creativity. When the increased testing requirements were implemented, the parents' association protested by keeping their children home on testing days.

The creation and implementation of the Common Core Learning Standards (CCLS) is national policy that impacts the lives of teachers and school leaders. Years in the making with the input of experts (mainly college educators) and selected teachers on each grade level and in each subject area, the Standards sought to ensure that students in every state graduated high school with the same base of knowledge.

Almost immediately there were problems. First, parents were only tangentially involved in the development of the Standards. Second, parents and even teachers found the language of the CCLS difficult to understand. Third, the Standards came with increased testing. Fourth, districts often took the CCLS, intended as guidelines, and made them into a rigid set of unit plans, even to creating standardized lessons (we will discuss this further in Chapter 7).

School leaders, such as Ms. Wren, who had little or nothing to do with the creation of the CCLS or implementation procedures, were left with the problems created. They had to deal with the backlash of parents and teachers while at the same time implementing the mandates of the CCLS. They frequently had to begin school-based implementation without knowing all the parameters or mandates for which they would be held accountable; sometimes, these parameters and mandates changed without warning.

Having national standards is nothing new—many countries around the world have been using them for decades, but with differences. Let's compare the US with Finland. The Finnish national standards for mathematics, grades 1 to 9, are ten pages long (Hancock 2011, 96). Teachers implement them based on their experience and individual teaching styles. The US Common Core math standards for grade 1 alone are thirteen pages long.

In Finland, there are no mandated standardized tests until grade 12. Tests are available after grade 6 but are optional (Hancock 2011, 99). In the US, testing has always been the norm, one expanded by the CCLS. Finland has a 2018 PISA math score of 507; the US, 478 (see Table 1.1).

There is a good reason for this: "Finland's schools are publicly funded. The people in the government agencies funding them, from national officials to local authorities are educators, not businesspeople, military leaders or politicians" (Hancock 2011, 96).

While there are social differences between the US and Finland that impact on pedagogical methods and student success, the US can learn much from the way schools are funded and curriculum developed and implemented.

Let's look at a national policy that has a not so obvious impact in classrooms—the lack of gun control legislation.

Elementary principal Ms. Wren was startled on the first day of school when several distraught parents were worried because their kindergarten students were assigned to a classroom on the first floor, in a corridor right off the main school entrance. They said that if there was an armed intruder, their children would be the first to die. A few months later, the same parents told her how the mandatory lockdown drills upset their five-year-olds.

In today's world, one cannot discuss factors affecting school success without addressing the issue of safety in an age of unbridled gun violence. There is fear in the classroom, not overt terror, but subconscious knowledge that at any time someone with a gun may wreak havoc in a school. This fear affects even the youngest child, who learns the reason for lockdown drills and hears reports of shootings blaring from televisions, radios, and internet sites.

The United States has a gun culture. The beacon of democracy was built on an ethos that espoused and glorified the use of firearms. America was born from a war and expanded using guns to exterminate the native population. It fought a civil war in which citizens used guns to kill each other. The US became a world power through the use of firearms in WWI and WWII.

Thirty percent of Americans say they own a gun; 42% say they live in a household with a gun (Gramlich and Schaeffer 2019). How did Americans respond to the COVID-19 virus? "Gun sellers across the United States are reporting major spikes in firearm and bullet purchases as the coronavirus spreads across the country. . . . The ammunition website Ammo.com said it has recorded an unprecedented surge in bullet sales" (Alcorn 2020). What was the federal government's response? According to an NRA lawsuit against New York State (which closed all gun stores) on March 28, the Department of Homeland Security issued a list of critical infrastructures, including "Workers supporting the operation of firearm or ammunition product manufacturers, retailers, importers, distributors, and shooting ranges" (Larson 2020).

Many of our cultural heroes used guns: frontiersmen, such as Davy Crockett gloriously dying as he shot the enemy at the Alamo; soldiers, such as Sergeant York, the pacifist expert in the use of arms; gunslingers and exploiters, such as Wyatt Earp and Buffalo Bill; and even antiheroes, as real as Al Capone, and fictional, as Vito Corleone. Guns are embedded in our cultural psych in a way that other civilized countries cannot understand. For the longest time, this culture stayed outside the school building. Columbine and Sandy Hook changed this forever.

Make no mistake: the main way to end school violence is by changing the attitude and cultural norms of this nation. This will take generations. Federal and state governments can create stringent gun control laws to reduce gun violence until the norm changes. Most do nothing. Some lawmakers espouse arming more citizens so they can use their weapons to take down perpetrators. They want us to go back to the streets of Laredo and Dodge City.

Legislators totally ignore the majority of citizens who feel some form of gun control is necessary. "A Pew Research Center survey conducted in September found that 60% of Americans say gun laws should be tougher, up from 57% last year and 52% in 2017" (Treisman 2019). "The latest NBC News-Wall Street Journal survey finds that 89 percent of Americans favor expanded background checks for gun purchasers, 76 percent support "red flag" laws to identify dangerous persons and deny them guns, and 75 percent favor a voluntary buyback program in which the government would purchase firearms from current owners. Sixty-two percent of Americans favor a ban on the sale of semi-automatic weapons" (Walsh 2019).

At the very least, all automatic weapons need to be banned from homes; all gun purchases must be made in person by someone who has a license to own a gun; anyone applying for a license to own a gun should have a thorough criminal and psychological background check. This is common sense, something lawmakers seem to lack.

Such regulations would not preclude gun enthusiasts from owning weapons. They could own automatic weapons, but these would have to be secured and used at a licensed gun range to prevent them falling into the wrong hands. Nonautomatic weapons would be stored at home in a locked, secure location inaccessible to unlicensed persons and subject to random police inspection.

Many will say this is an intrusion on privacy. Let's for the moment look at another practice—adopting a pet from a shelter. If you've ever done this, you know that you need to complete a lengthy form and submit letters attesting to your character. Then, before you adopt, a background check is done to be sure you would not be a cruel pet owner. In some states, homes are visited to be sure the pet would not be mistreated. Should owning a gun be easier than adopting a pet from a shelter?

Let's see what the states have done regarding schools and gun control. In twenty-two states, weapons in schools are explicitly prohibited.

Nine states permit the carrying of concealed weapons in school, and some, such as Alabama and Oregon, have no restrictions other than that the carrier be licensed. Others, such as Missouri and South Dakota, limit concealed weapons to designated school administrators or teachers. Michigan allows the carrying of a concealed weapon in a school by any person licensed in any state, provided the principal gives permission (Education Commission of the States 2019). It would seem that state legislatures are no better than Washington in dealing with gun control—or other issues pertaining to education.

The Tenth Amendment to the United States Constitution provides that most education policy is decided at the state or local level. The influence of state politicos varies from state to state. We know states can augment financing provided by local school districts. This is a common practice, although many states were forced into it by court decisions requiring them to provide an equitable education for all students.

Some state policies, however, take money away from schools. Let's look at state laws regarding homeschooling and charter schools.

According to the Coalition for Responsible Home Education, a homeschooling advocacy group, in the 2015–2016 school year, 1,690,000 children were homeschooled, or 3.3% of the school-age population. The same source charts the highest level of education of the parents of homeschooled children: 15% have not earned a high school diploma; 16% have a high school diploma or its equivalent; 25% have vocational/technical training or some college; 30% have a bachelor's degree; 15% have a graduate or professional degree (Coalition for Responsible Home Education n.d.).

The majority of parents homeschool themselves. It is probably a safe assumption that at least 55% of instruction is provided by poorly prepared parents. How is this possible? The Home School Legal Defense Association (HSLDA), another advocacy group, provides parents interested in homeschooling with information on how to home educate children. It provides a color-coded map of the US with each state designated as having low, moderate, or high regulation.

Eleven states require "no notice" (HSLDA n.d.). What does this mean? In general, parents in these states are not even required to notify governmental authorities that they are homeschooling, at least according to the HSLDA. There are, however, a range of requirements in the different states.

Idaho has no requirements for the instructors' qualifications, requires no school district approval, has no required testing; homeschooling parents or their designees are not required to furnish any information to the district but must teach the subjects usually taught in the public schools.

In Connecticut, parents are not required to initiate contact with government officials before beginning homeschooling but must teach required subjects. Indiana considers homeschooling as a "non-accredited private school." Instruction must be in English; the same number of instructional days as public schools is required; attendance records must be kept; information on the homeschooling may be requested by the district or state.

There is a great deal of variation in the fifteen states designated by the HSLDA as having "low regulation." In Mississippi there are no teaching qualifications, no standardized testing, no required subjects or required instructional days. In Kansas, the instructor must be "competent"; no subjects are required. But instruction must be planned and scheduled, and the child must be tested periodically. Delaware law provides three options for homeschooling, none requiring any teacher qualifications or standardized testing (HSLDA n.d.).

In summary, twenty-six states have minimal homeschooling regulations. Most homeschooled students are taught by parents or designees lacking teaching certification or even a college degree. Beyond our concern for the education and socialization of children, why is this important to school districts and schools?

In a few paragraphs, we will be discussing district funding formulas, based on student enrollment. Taking 1,690,000 students out of the public schools reduces student enrollment. Depending on the state and district, this means localities do not have to pay for 80,000 to 100,000 certified teachers nationwide. To look at it another way, on average, district resources are decreased by the 3.3%.

If we go back to the premise that spending less money is a motivating factor for politicians, this is money they do not have to spend on education in their states. Saving money and not alienating homeschooling parents and their advocacy groups is more important than ensuring the appropriate education of children.

A financial motivation does not overtly apply to state policies regarding charter schools. First, let's look at the numbers. Forty-four states and the District of Columbia have laws regarding charter schools (Education Commission of the States 2020).

Twenty states have no cap on the number of charter schools, but there may be some provisos. For example, in Delaware a local school board may limit the number of charter school applications or approvals. In Missouri, charter schools may be opened only in designated areas (e.g., a metropolitan school district).

Some states with a cap are more generous in allowing new schools than others. California, for example, allowed 250 charter schools to open in the 1998–1999 school year—and allows up to fifty more to open in each subsequent year (Education Commission of the States 2018).

The debate over the efficacy of charter schools continues to rage along with allegations of financial improprieties. The bottom line is simple. There are successful charter schools, just as there are successful public schools. There are failing charter schools, just as there are failing public schools. There is some misuse of monies in all types of schools. All schools can learn from the successful practices of other schools. Student success rates seem to be the same for both types of schools.

There is a downside to charter schools funded by the state or district. In either case, this is less money going to public schools. Some of this money is supporting students who would be in public schools; some is excess. If the children went to their designated public school or, if permitted, the public school of choice, there would be no need to fund the cost of a principal and administrative overhead of a separate charter school. This would be a saving of several hundred thousand dollars per charter school, a saving that could be used by the districts to enhance programs in the public school.

In addition, charter schools that occupy a separate building have maintenance and custodial costs. Those sharing spaces with traditional public schools put restrictions on the use of common spaces and inhibit creative programming possibilities for the public schools.

So why are some state lawmakers enamored of charter schools? Charter schools have strong lobbying groups, often claiming to represent a significant portion of the electorate. They know how to brand themselves. They allow politicians to say they are promoting educational innovation without allocating more state funds—they simply shift them from public school budgets.

State policies and laws regarding homeschooling and charter schools diminish the funding public schools could use to better serve students.

Principal candidate Joaquin researched the needs of a poverty-stricken neighborhood in a large urban city. He was born and lived there. He went to community meetings to discuss his plan for a new school that would address the needs of the neighborhood children. He had intense and enthusiastic support from the community and submitted his proposal for this new school to the district. The district approved the school, but located it in a different neighborhood across town. Mr. Joaquin reached out to this new community but, as an outsider, could not get the support of the parents or community. In a few years, the school failed and was subsumed into another school housed in the same building.

School districts are supposed to support schools, teachers, and school-based leaders. Most do. Yet more and more school districts are political animals, bowing to the wishes of school boards, local community and parent organizations, local politicians, and other pressure groups. In Mr. Joaquin's case, political placement of his school led to its failure.

A recent poll of district-level administrators and school principals conducted by *Education Week* confirms some of these influences. Those surveyed were asked which group represents the biggest obstacle to making spending decisions that best address their students' needs. The top responses were:

- State legislators, 51%
- Local superintendents of schools and central office staff, 12%
- Federal legislators, 11%
- Local school board members, 10% ("We Asked About School Finance. What Did Districts Say?" 2019, 3)

Respondents were then asked to use the standard A to F grades to rate the understanding of various groups regarding their district's or school's funding needs. Some responses were:

- Federal elected officials: 29% F; 33% D
- State elected officials: 19% F; 31% D
- The US Department of Education: 25% F; 28% D

- Local elected officials: 13% F; 25% D ("We Asked About School Finance. What Did Districts Say?" 2019, 4)

Such poor regard for the different groups is the result of decisions about schools being made by bureaucrats and noneducators whose main priority might not be students or schools.

Another example is the curricular interference of local school boards. Until recently, when the courts overturned their policies, some school boards in several states insisted on a curriculum that required creationism be taught along with evolution as an equally valid theory. A few prohibited the term "climate change" from being used in instruction. Such political and religious views have no place in the public school classroom, yet it took years of court battles to overturn them.

Shortly after her appointment as an assistant principal, Ms. Rayne had a visit from her superintendent. She did not like the texts being used and directed that Ms. Rayne use a set of textbooks that she favored. The superintendent provided funding for this purchase. Ms. Rayne, with the principal's approval, purchased the new texts and arranged for her teachers to have PD in their use. She created a curriculum committee for each grade level so each could devise a lesson calendar and unit plans aligned with the new texts.

By September of the next year everything was ready for full implementation. The superintendent was removed. The new superintendent did not like these texts, feeling they lacked rigor. She told Ms. Rayne to phase them out in favor of different books. Eight months later, there was another new superintendent with different ideas. Ms. Rayne and her staff were totally demoralized.

There is a high turnover rate of school superintendents. The American Association of School Administrators reports that the average tenure of a superintendent is five to six years; the turnover rate 14% to 16% per year (American Association of School Administrators 2006). This is a challenge to continuity of leadership, as we see in assistant principal Rayne's inability to implement a curriculum.

A child entering kindergarten is likely to have three or more superintendents before graduating high school, each with his or her own educational priorities and each answering to the whims of periodically elected school boards and politicians. This makes it difficult to create a seamless K–12 curricula.

Is it any wonder that school-based leaders and teachers are indifferent about implementing educational innovations mandated from superintendents? They feel this year's innovation will be next year's anathema. Experience tells them that time devoted to changing plans and pedagogy to meet new mandates will most likely be wasted, as these mandates will change in one or two years. How can principals, who need the trust of their teachers to lead schools, insist on compliance with what they know will surely change?

Principal Wren had a mantra that she repeated at her opening meeting with her staff every September: "Good teaching is good teaching." She knew that each year the terminology and emphasis might change but that caring teachers who achieved good results with their students need not abandon the successful strategies and methods they always used—just tweak them to satisfy "the powers that be." When she believed a new initiative was of value, she worked with her teachers to integrate it into their pedagogy, expanding their repertoires, not replacing the fine strategies they had used for years.

Districts and superintendents can do good work. The support they provided to students parents, teachers, and principals during the COVID-19 pandemic is an excellent example. They worked tirelessly to ease the transition to distance learning. They listened to constituencies when problems arose and modified policies. Unfortunately, several school systems caved in to political pressures as the crisis continued. They chose to prematurely open schools, gambling with the health and safety of students, staff and families.

Large and midsize school districts develop policies to ensure that principals implement good fiscal practices in their schools and not spend beyond their allocated budget. This sounds simple but involves a complex interplay of many variables.

Tax levy budget allocations are often based on projected student enrollments. To give a simple example: if the contractual number of pupils of a middle school classroom is twenty-eight and each teacher has five classes, then you need an allocation of seven teachers (English, mathematics, science, social studies, LOTE, PE, and either computer science or art or music) for every 140 students.

Or not, as some classes, such as computer science, art/music, CTE, and PE might have higher or lower class sizes and/or meet fewer (or more) than five times a week. The smaller the school, the more difficult it is to ensure that each class is maximized. If there are seventy-two sixth-grade students, for instance, the average class size would be twenty-four, not twenty-eight, costing more dollars per student. Let's say, as an example, that, based on class sizes, the number of periods per week, and a less-than-contractual class size, a school needs an allocation of one teacher for every twenty students.

But a school needs support staff as well—a principal, assistant principals, guidance counselors, secretaries, school aides, and security personnel. In most districts, this is considered administrative overhead and receives a separate allocation in addition to that given for instruction. The number of students in the school is still a consideration. The fewer the students, the fewer assistant principals, secretaries, counselors, and aides needed.

Some students are programmed for additional support for a variety of reasons: they have special needs, their first language is not English, they need gifted and talented enrichment, they have deficiencies in reading or mathematics. Federal Title I and Title VII funding helps with some of this; however, the needs of the gifted and talented are often ignored, and it is up to the school to fund programs for them out of their regular allocation.

Taking all this into consideration, let's say that the student-to-teacher ratio is 14:1. In terms of money, this would mean that, for every fourteen students in the school, the school allocation would increase by the average salary (plus benefits) of one teacher in the school. So, if the average salary were $50,000 and the benefit package (sick days, medical coverage, maternity/paternity allowances, and pension contributions) were $25,000, every 14 students would yield an allocation of $75,000; 140 students, an allocation of $750,000; and 1,400 students, $7,500,000.

All of the above is oversimplified, as there are other allocations and grants that go into a school budget. The essential concept is that enrollment drives budget. Usually, every spring, a principal projects enrollment for the coming fall so that the allocation can be determined. Underestimate, and the school receives less than it should; overestimate, and the school receives more.

When a school over- or underestimates, principals can often send a revised enrollment estimate before a fall cutoff date to return funds or claim additional monies. Either way, the programming of the school is disrupted as teaching positions and classes are added or subtracted.

If a school underestimates and does not ask for more funds, the school just makes do with the original allocation; if a school overestimates and does not return funds, however, it may be penalized the following school year by having funds subtracted from its computed allocation. This is a nice way of saying that the students and school will suffer because the principal made a mistake.

Even this is a simplification. In the example above, let's say a principal in a school of 2,800 overestimates by 2%, or 56 students. This would be a penalty of $300,000, or the equivalent of four teachers. Estimates can be affected by many factors beyond the control of the school, such as population shifts and perceived property values around the school. The actual allocation given each year can vary, depending on whether the citizens of the district vote to raise or lower property taxes.

An enlightened district might have a credit/debit system. A school that underestimates one year gets a credit for future use in case it overestimates.

However, as school district budgets are determined by a vote on property taxes each year, the district may not able to project if they have the money to cover such a credit.

Newly assigned principal, Mr. Joaquin, was distraught over his budget allocation for the next school year. Only 58% of the students in his middle school qualified for free or reduced lunch. In his urban district, 60% were required to have a Title I School Wide Program. To make matters worse, his predecessor had overstated the school's enrollment, and the school had received a higher allocation the previous year than it should have. The district was now penalizing the school by reducing its budget to "pay back" what was owed. He and his staff struggled with the budget to provide programs for students in need of academic support while maintaining enrichment and elective programs for other students.

Mr. Joaquin's predecessor did a poor job. Because he or she did not tenaciously collect lunch applications and overestimated enrollment, Mr. Joaquin finds himself in his first year as principal facing a significant fiscal shortfall that could reduce teaching staff and programs. Unless an enlightened superintendent steps in and provides the monies lost from the district's discretionary funds, this new principal will begin in dire straits which, through no fault of his own, could lead to poor student performance and his own dismissal.

Principal Joaquin and his wife were thrilled when the mayor expanded Universal Pre-K so that their daughter would be able to attend school the coming September in the same building as her older brother, reducing their childcare costs. However, they discovered that there was very limited space in the school. Parents would be given a choice of four possible locations (one their district designated school) and, through a lottery, have their pre-K child assigned to a school.

As it turned out, Mr. and Mrs. Joaquin were not given any of their choices due to lack of space. Their daughter was assigned to a pre-K site a mile and a half from their son's school. They went to the district office but were told it was the only space available. Mrs. Joaquin was able to continue to drop off her son while Mr. Joaquin could pick him up, but, because their daughter started and ended her day at the same times as their son, they had to hire a childcare provider to accompany her to and from school.

The policies and decisions of local school leaders can impact districts and children. In 2014, Bill de Blasio's New York City mayoral campaign stressed the expansion of the Universal Prekindergarten Program. Once elected, the program expanded exponentially with little consideration for spaces available.

Let's look at the Joaquins' problem. Their local elementary school had six kindergarten classes (two rented from a nearby religious school), so it could be assumed they would need at least six pre-K classrooms. The already filled to capacity school was able to find space for only one pre-K room. This scenario played out in scores of elementary schools throughout New York City.

Spaces were found in underutilized parochial, Yeshiva, and private schools; in office buildings; in district offices; and in unused firehouse spaces. Existing private and religious affiliated preschools, which agreed to adhere to Department of Education guidelines, were designated as approved pre-Ks and received funding. But parents were left with logistical problems and extra childcare costs.

There also was a severe shortage of licensed pre-K teachers and minimal oversight of the instruction delivered outside the regular school buildings. Universal Pre-K is a positive, but districts, schools, and parents should not be left with the logistical and oversight burdens caused by a political decision that neglected to plan for the basic needs of space and teachers.

Districts can also have conflicting policies that make a principal's job virtually impossible. School safety is a priority for any principal, but district policy can turn this priority into a nightmare.

Let's look at the current policies of a large urban school district. Principals (or their designees) must report any incidents of corporal punishment, verbal abuse, bullying, or cyberbullying. Incident reports must be completed within a short time frame and called in or emailed to an appropriate investigatory department. In almost all cases, the principal is told to investigate, complete a report, and submit it within a few days. An investigation will include record reviews and interviews of students, parents, and teachers (the latter within contractual limits, often permitting teachers to have representation).

This gets carried further. An anonymous call to the district office will be referred back to the principal of the school reported for him or her to investigate. Any parent who feels that a child is bullied can directly report this allegation to the district office, circumventing the principal entirely, even though the principal will be told to investigate. The definition of "bullying" includes a single incident where the child felt bullied. Not only must the allegation be investigated, but an individualized support program must be devised for both the bullied child and the bully.

Principals and other members of the supervisory staff are becoming on-site investigatory agencies. At the same time, they are told that they must be the instructional leaders and spend most of their time in classrooms supporting instruction and advising teachers.

School-based leaders and teachers have no control over the mandates from the government and district. These change frequently. Often, there is little or no funding for implementation. As with the implementation of CCLS, they may embroil the school, which had no say or control over the policy, in controversy with angry parents.

School-based leaders and teachers are subject to a lack of continuity and vision from entities outside of the school. They have little control over budget allocations and may face penalties from even minor fluctuations in enrollment. Newly assigned principals may find themselves paying for the follies of their predecessors.

Principals and teachers can organize protests at government and district offices. This will get them a sound bite on the media for a few hours but the time and effort put into the organization of the protest will have little if any impact—and take them away from instruction in the school.

Have the evaluators of schools taken the impact of "the powers that be" into their matrices for determining school success? Do they calculate the monies lost to schools due to homeschooling or the program restrictions caused by the housing of charter schools in the same buildings with public schools? Are they aware of how fear affects children and parents in our age of gun violence—or how much money a school must now spend on security to prevent such violence? Do they have a statistic on how much of a school-based leader's time is spent on investigatory matters, rather than the development and supervision of staff?

Chapter Three

The School Building

When Ms. Rayne became AP in a large urban high school, she quickly became aware of potentially serious issues with the student lockers. In her circa-1940 building, "locker areas" were located in isolated corners on most floors. More lockers were located in the back of each classroom. The locker corners were student hangouts for smoking and romantic liaisons. Theft was a problem. The locker metal had deteriorated so that students could pull out the rear panel and have access to an adjacent locker's contents.

Over time, Ms. Rayne's principal had all the corner lockers removed. A front wall with a door was added to each area creating storage space for books and materials. Students used the classroom lockers. Since the school was on overlapping sessions, this led to classroom disruptions during the first and last two periods of the school day.

When Ms. Rayne became principal, she lobbied the district for new lockers to be placed along the walls of the very wide hallways. For five years she tried to get these lockers, to no avail. By chance, a member of her PA sat on the district PA, and a member of the student government sat on the district student board. Both of them, with the support of their membership, joined the campaign with the principal. Within two years, new lockers lined the halls of the school. The custodian bolted the classroom lockers, leaving a few available for teacher use.

It took over fifteen years to solve the locker problems. The solutions led to fewer incidents and eliminated classroom locker disruptions.

School facilities are important, as noted in a recent *Kappan* article: "Decades of research confirm that the conditions and qualities of school facilities affect students, teachers, and overall academic achievement" (Filardo, Vincent, and Sullivan 2019, 28).

This chapter has two sections. The first will focus on the physical plant of the school building, a factor often omitted when judging a school's effectiveness and over which school leaders and teachers have minimal control. The second will look at the location of the building and its effect on attracting and retaining teachers. Money impacts on both the physical plant and its location.

There are at least eighteen physical plant factors that have positive or negative influence on student and school success. Within very limited parameters, knowing what they are may help school leaders make decisions regarding school safety, personnel, and budget. They may also guide principals regarding where they might need the support of parents and students to lobby districts for change.

The first eleven factors concern the design of the school:

(1) Our stereotypic image of a school building is that of a temple of learning. As we approach, we see classic lines, maybe a Greek portico, perhaps a dome or tower. Inside, we see marble hallways, display cases with trophies, and classrooms with high ceilings and large windows for natural lighting. Such buildings, most of which were built prior to WWII and many through Roosevelt's Works Project Administration, are architectural gems. They impress students, staff, and parents who enter, sending a clear message: these are serious places designed for serious learning.

Beginning in the 1960s, utilitarianism and parsimony trumped impressiveness and beauty, ushering in the era of cinder block schools that lack the gravitas of older buildings. Sadly, many of the grand old schools fell into disrepair due to lack of funds, overcrowding, and poor maintenance. Instead of impressing, they became symbols of infrastructure neglect.

An overlooked aspect of education is the aesthetic appeal of the building—what message does the building itself send to students, parents, and staff?

(2) Whether old or new, it is clear that school architects may not have always sought or heeded the input of educators. Low-storied buildings designed in a U-shape or square are the easiest for school administration to monitor. During changes of class a staff member stationed in each corner on each floor can control the flow of students.

The more floors, the more adults needed. A school built with interior corridors crossing the building at two, three, or even four places, dramatically increases the number of adults needed for monitoring. This is the first of several examples we will see where the need for security in our complex world may drain resources that could otherwise be used for instruction.

(3) Space for teachers, parents, and student study halls may be limited. Teacher collaboration is fundamental for shared leadership and professional development, but utilitarian buildings sometimes leave little space for subject or grade-level teacher centers. It is difficult to convert classroom spaces to

such centers because of district regulations concerning school capacity (see #12). It could also be argued that schools should have adult-monitored student centers providing safe spaces for students to socialize and study. Finally, can the school accommodate a parent center?

(4) The more entrances/exits a school has and the larger the campus, the more personnel needed to monitor student comings and goings. In almost all cases, this number is mandated by fire codes to ensure the building may be emptied quickly and safely during an emergency.

Today school leaders must be vigilant regarding dangerous intruders, multiple exterior doors are a security risk. Panic bars with loud alarms and video monitors at rarely used doors help but will not prevent an in-school accomplice from opening a door and allowing an intruder into the building. On-site personnel could prevent such an accomplice from acting, but adult monitors, whether security guards, school aides, or teachers, cost money.

Schools with large campuses that include athletic fields have even more areas needing security.

(5) It seems like common sense to house major school offices in as few suites as possible to make it easier for students and parents to confer with counselors, deans, and department chairs, all located in proximate areas. The need for security requires a different design. Disaggregated offices placed near doors and corner areas provide additional adult monitoring of entrances and hallways at no additional cost. The original school design, room size, and the location of retaining walls might prevent such disaggregation.

(6) When one's personal space is invaded, one becomes nervous, tense, and more apt to act inappropriately. Wide hallways and stairwells help prevent this; narrow ones exacerbate it. Each school's spatial problem is unique, depending on its design and the building code at the time it was built.

(7) This follows from the above. With wide enough hallways, student lockers can be placed in hallways, rather than classrooms, eliminating the need for "locker periods" at the beginning and end of the day, adding instructional time and eliminating the interruption of instruction when students need to enter a classroom to retrieve a book or gym shorts.

(8) Room size is another personal space issue. Some middle and high schools are housed in buildings originally intended for elementary students, so the room proportions needed for older students are inappropriate. Some schools are housed in office buildings where the rooms were never intended to be used as classrooms.

Often, rooms are just too small for the contractual class size. In older schools, built when wooden right hand–only desks were nailed to the floor, modern moveable furniture takes up more space than the rooms were designed for. How many classroom dustups are caused by poor desk arrangement exacerbated by space limitations? How much budgetary flexibility is lost because fewer than the contractual number of students can be safely seated in a small room? How many students will a principal be able to fit in such rooms if social distancing regulations are imposed?

(9) A school area prone to incidents is the cafeteria. If the cafeteria has any shape other than a square, rectangle, or circle, additional personnel will be needed for supervision. For example, a U-shaped cafeteria, with the service area at the bottom of the U is essentially two separate rooms needing adult supervision.

If the lunchroom is too small, the school will be forced to have four, five, or even six lunch periods in an eight- or nine-period day, putting early ones close to breakfast and late ones near dismissal, denying students a break toward the middle of the day. The more lunch periods, the more funds needed to pay for security and supervision, the less money for instruction. Social distancing could increase the number of lunch periods necessary and perhaps require the use of adjacent classrooms to provide additional space.

Finally, good food makes everyone feel better. Cafeterias with full cooking facilities will serve better fare than those that can serve only warmed-up precooked deliveries, with the ambience and taste of TV dinners. Students given a freshly made lunch are more likely to enjoy the meal and socialize, rather than disrupt. They also will have a healthier diet.

(10) Those schools housed in buildings not intended as schools often have no gyms. Administration usually finds the largest room available and uses it for gym alternatives, such as dance or yoga. There are at least two drawbacks to this. First, students are denied choice—no basketball, volleyball, calisthenics, or gymnastics. Second, fewer students can be accommodated for PE than allowed by contract, forcing the use of extra school resources that could have been used for academics.

Lack of appropriate spaces affects other subject areas. Does the school have a music room? An art room? Rooms for CTE classes? Even with the current emphasis on STEAM, the arts occupy the lowest rung on the instructional totem pole but are important if students are to have a well-rounded education.

Many inner-city schools lack athletic fields, so they use nearby public park space or the facilities of their more suburban cousins. This has at least four drawbacks. First, scheduling issues limit practice time. Second, home games are never played at the school itself. Third, onlookers tend to be from the opposing team's school because travel outside the campus is inconvenient. Fourth, the school's team is always traveling somewhere, increasing its time to get home and reducing study time.

(11) Every principal tries to avoid the dreaded whole school assembly. However, sometimes there is a need to speak to the entire student body at

once, address incoming students and their parents, and have special events as awards or performance evenings. An internal auditorium also serves as a secure space for mandated shelter drills or real emergencies. Many schools lack a large auditorium. Some were built this way to save space; others, housed in what were originally office buildings, have no space. Just having an auditorium is not enough—to be of value to the school and students, it must have appropriate lighting, audio, and video systems.

There is not much school leaders can do about school design. They can be creative in monitoring entrances/exits with a variable combination of panic bars, cameras, and personnel. They can relocate offices, if such spaces can be refitted. Depending on the size of the room and number of students, they can use only one part of the lunchroom, easing monitoring. If hallways are wide enough, they can petition the district for the installation of hallway lockers and the dismantling of those in classrooms, as Ms. Rayne did in the anecdote at the beginning of this chapter. They may even be able to alter classroom size as long as weight-bearing walls are left intact.

The next three factors concern building use:

(12) When a school is built, it is given a student capacity number. Alterations or additions to the building change this number. It is difficult to convert classroom spaces to teacher meeting spaces or parent rooms because this reduces capacity, something few districts want to approve.

A key for the principal is not to exceed the designated capacity. This can be difficult, especially for schools in areas where there are insufficient buildings or for schools that have a high success rate so that more students opt to attend. A school leader needs to lobby for the school not to be oversized so that spatial problems already caused by building design are not exacerbated.

Overcrowding in school buildings is often caused by the district's failure to plan. When planning the construction of new buildings, districts must pay careful attention to population trends so that schools are not built for the present but for five or ten years in the future. The New York City Department of Education failed to do this in the 1970s, building schools in the borough of Manhattan when projected population growth was going to be in the outer boroughs, especially Queens.

The result? By the 1990s Queens schools were overcrowded while some Manhattan schools were underutilized. More elementary and middle schools had to be built in Queens, and, even today, many high schools operate on double or even triple sessions.

(13) Is it better for students to attend a middle or high school in their own neighborhood or travel to a larger magnet school? There are arguments for both sides. The neighborhood school minimizes travel time, reducing lateness;

is more accessible to parents; can adapt to the cultural needs of the community; and can often count on support from community organizations. A major downside, particularly in urban areas, is that the problems of the community, such as gangs, more easily come into the school. Issues between students that developed in earlier grades advance into the middle and high schools.

Magnate schools, drawing from different surrounding neighborhoods or communities, reduce these negatives. The past is forgotten as students have fresh starts in new places. Magnate schools often have special themes or programs, giving students a choice that may match their particular needs and interests. As they progress, they can choose from a variety of electives that mesh with their changing visions of their futures. Finally, students will be exposed to classmates of different ethnicities and cultures, widening their views of the world beyond their local neighborhoods. The downside is travel time for students and parents.

The chance for a child to have a fresh start in a new building where he or she has a choice of program and is exposed to the wider world trumps travel time.

Suburban and rural schools do not have this dilemma, as students travel to central campuses. This requires a fleet of school buses, drivers, and attendants. They can be direct employees or employees of a contracted company. Either way, a significant part of the district budget must be earmarked for transportation. Having dozens of children on a bus, even with a trained attendant, provides opportunities for light-hearted antics but also bullying and violence. Should there be trained security personnel on each bus?

(14) In urban and suburban areas there is a movement to downsize schools to allow for more personalization. This has led to several schools being located in a building where previously one large school had been unsuccessful. Three or more schools in a building creates problems with time schedules, shared spaces (library, gym, cafeteria, auditorium, entrances, and exits), mandated drills, and use of classroom space. Unhealthy competition between different student bodies could be problematic. If elementary, middle, and/or high schools are housed in one building, other issues may arise. There are ways to reduce all these problems, and schools have become adept at doing so with varying degrees of success.

Other issues cannot be dismissed so easily. Multiple schools in one building cost the district additional administrative overhead. Instead of paying for one principal and one principal's secretary, they are paying for three or more. Grade-level and subject-area supervision suffers, as smaller schools have fewer chairs or assistant principals. One "AP Everything" certified in mathematics may be supervising science, English, social studies, foreign language, and PE teachers. In an elementary school, an AP with a background in early childhood education may be supervising the fourth, fifth and even sixth grades.

This can have a devastating effect on student outcomes. Modern curricula require certified, knowledgeable grade-level and subject-area supervisors who can train staff in the pedagogy specific to each level or subject to ensure proper instruction and appropriately completed teacher evaluations. This issue can be addressed if all the schools on the same level in one building share department chairs so each grade level or subject area is supervised by a school leader certified in that area. Given the inevitable turf issues, this rarely is done.

The next three factors deal with school facilities:

(15) Many older, nonupgraded school buildings have antiquated heating systems and electrical wiring not suitable for air-conditioning. Newer buildings are not exempt, as poor construction practices may compromise these same systems. Student and staff comfort in all seasons is conducive to better teaching and learning. Principals need to be advocates for all the upgrades necessary—and superintendents need to support them at budgetary hearings.

(16) You cannot implement a STEAM-rich curriculum if you have antiquated lab facilities or no science labs, art studio, or music/band rooms. You cannot provide modern instruction in any area without technology laboratories (for specialized instruction in design, engineering, etc.) and in-class technology (e.g., smart boards, laptops, electronic texts). Schools located in low-income areas will also need computer centers where students without access to computers or internet at home can complete assignments, with a teacher monitor present, of course. Unbelievably costly!

Principals, teachers, parents, and superintendents must unite to fight for the facilities needed. Whether you are a techie or technophobe, schools must upgrade. This is also an income inequality issue, with affluent districts being able to provide far more for students and staff than districts in areas of poverty.

(17) Students often come to school with chronic medical problems (e.g., asthma and allergies), and some acute ones, such as the cold that gets suddenly worse. There are issues with eating disorders, birth control, and depression. Students sometimes get injured at school, tripping in a stairwell or getting hit by a basketball in gym.

A school that has a medical office with a full-time registered nurse and physician on call has a great advantage: instead of sending students home or to an emergency room, many medical problems can be treated on-site with the student returning to the classroom. The only expense to the school might be the creation of such an office, as some major hospitals trying to reduce the strain on their emergency rooms are willing to provide staff without cost.

Finally, there is the one important factor of school maintenance:

(18) Regardless of the age or condition of the physical plant, everyone in the building can work together to keep the school clean, a home away from home. This is the one area where school leaders and staff have the most control.

Principals are focused on instruction, but teaching and learning are enhanced by good ambience. They need to take seriously any part they play in the ratings of custodians. Custodians are more likely to do their jobs well if they see that school leaders work with students and staff to keep classrooms and hallways clean by using the appropriate trash and recycle receptacles. This will involve training students, particularly those new to the school. It will also involve staff in establishing end-of-day cleanup procedures in their classrooms.

All these factors are summarized in Table 3.1.

Much of the above is related to what governments refer to as "capital spending," that is, monies allocated to the maintenance and upgrading of existing buildings and the construction of new ones. There is never enough money. The Center on Budget and Policy Priorities reports that, nationwide, capital spending on K–12 schools fell from about 80 billion dollars in 2008 to just under 60 billion in 2016, a drop of 25%.

Adjusted for inflation, this varies significantly from state to state. In Nevada, for example, the capital spending from 2008 to 2016 decreased by 81%; Florida, 71%; Arizona, 70%; Delaware, 62%; Vermont, 55%; North Carolina, 53%. Only two states increased spending, Washington by 9% and Montana by 12%. A few were well below the average decrease of 25%: Arkansas, 1%; Oregon, 2%; Indiana, 7%; Texas, 9%; New York, Kentucky, and New Mexico, 14% (Leachman 2018).

In 2012–2013, the National Center for Educational Statistics surveyed a nationally representative sample of school districts and reported: "Based on survey responses, 53 percent of public schools needed to spend money on repairs, renovations, and modernizations to put the school's onsite buildings in good overall condition. . . . The total amount needed was estimated to be approximately $197 billion, and the average dollar amount for schools needing to spend money was about $4.5 million per school." (Alexander and Lewis 2014).

School leaders cannot fret over what they cannot change. Most aspects of a school's physical plant are just givens and can be changed only by government spending, controlled by the "powers that be."

"Poor communities whose school facilities need the most attention have typically received the least facility funding, as seen in a national study of more than 146,000 school facility improvement projects from 1995 to 2004 which found that projects located in high-wealth zip codes had more than three times the capital investment than schools in the lowest-wealth zip codes" (Filardo, Vincent, and Sullivan 2019, 29).

Once again, we see the negative effect of poverty and income inequality. Students who could benefit most from upgraded facilities receive the least at the local and district level. Perhaps local leaders and district superintendents

Table 3.1. School Building Factors That Impact on School Success

	Category	Tending to Have a Positive Impact	Tending to Have a Negative Impact
1	Building Design	Aesthetically appealing, such as many well maintained schools built prior to WWII	Not aesthetically appealing, such as cinder block schools or older schools in disrepair
2	Building Design	Simple design (square, U-shape)	Complex design with interior corridors and secluded areas
3	Building Design	Defined spaces for teachers, parents, and student study rooms	Few or no such defined spaces
4	Building Design	Six or fewer entrances/egresses	Seven or more entrances/egresses
5	Building Design	Offices placed in key locations to allow for greater monitoring of students	Offices are clustered in one or two areas
6	Building Design	Wide hallways	Narrow hallways
7	Building Design	Lockers in hallways	Lockers in classrooms
8	Building Design	Room size appropriate for number of students assigned and the age of the students	Room size inappropriate
9	Building Design	Cafeteria • One large room • On-site cooking facilities • Large enough to accommodate at least one-third of the student body	Cafeteria: • More than one room or space • Only facilities for heating up food • So small four or more lunch periods are needed
10	Building Design	Has gymnasium and athletic fields	Does not have gymnasium and/or athletic fields
11	Building Design	Auditorium large enough to hold the entire student body	No auditorium or too small an auditorium
12	Building Use	At or below stated student capacity	Over the stated student capacity
13	Building Use Middle/High School	Magnate school	Neighborhood school
14	Building Use	Single school in building	Multiple schools in building
15	School Facilities	AC/heating appropriate	AC/heating inappropriate
16	School Facilities	Has sufficient science and technology labs, etc.	Does not have sufficient science and technology labs, etc.
17	School Facilities	Has a medical office	Does not have a medical office
18	Building Maintenance	Well maintained with cooperation of the custodian, staff, and students	Not well maintained through custodial neglect and/or lack of staff and student support

do not realize the relationship between student achievement and the physical plant. Perhaps they have decided that some schools will not succeed and choose to assign capital funds to those schools that give them high achievement scores. Maybe they feel that money spent on schools in districts beset by poverty will be lost due to vandalism and theft. Whatever the reason, poverty and income inequality are affecting the very buildings in which students learn and teachers teach.

The problem goes deeper.

When Ms. Wren was looking for her first teaching position, she researched schools and found a school in a poverty-stricken area that had good statistics and high ratings from parents. She submitted her resume and was called for an interview. When she got off the bus at the nearest stop, she found the streets were littered with syringes. Storefronts were boarded up, and buildings were covered with gang-related graffiti. Vagrants were sitting or lying in doorways.

She went for the interview but felt that the four-block walk to the school would be unsafe, particularly when daylight savings time ended and she would be going home in the dark. Years later, when she was looking for a supervisory position, Ms. Wren found that the school was on the verge of being phased out due to poor student achievement.

Students entering Ms. Rayne's culinary and hospitality themed magnet urban high school often had low scores in ELA and mathematics; the percentage of entering students who were ELL and special needs paralleled the percentages entering nonmagnet high schools. The school was located in a low-crime business district of the city, with amenities such as a Whole Foods Market on one corner and a Starbucks on the other. Upscale stores, gyms, bistros, and cafes were within easy walking distance, and the school itself was one block away from bus and rapid transit stops. She had no problem recruiting and retaining teachers. Eighty-eight percent of the students met graduation requirements four years after they entered, well above the district average.

Studies indicate that it is difficult to retain teachers in low-income schools. For example, 56.4% of Teach for America teachers leave their initial job placements in low-income schools after two years; by their fifth year, only 14.8% continue in their original assignment (Donaldson and Moore 2011).

Other studies "suggest that teachers who leave high-poverty schools are not fleeing their students. Rather, they are fleeing the poor working conditions that make it difficult for them to teach and for their students to learn" (Simon and Moore Johnson 2015). Teachers and principals, such as Ms. Wren and Ms. Rayne, might feel that the issue of working conditions has more to do with the surrounding neighborhood than conditions within the school.

"The Effect of School Neighborhoods on Teacher Career Decisions" states "little work assesses the extent to which differences in the neighborhoods in which schools are located either affect teacher recruitment and retention or explain the observed relationship between school characteristics and teachers' career choices" (Boyd et al. 2010, 1).

Boyd et al. note: "In applying to schools, teachers tend to favor neighborhoods with higher median family income and less violent crime. In higher-density areas, teachers also favor neighborhoods with greater local amenities, particularly amenities for practical (grocery, hardware, drug stores) and leisure (bars, fitness centers, coffee shops, movie theaters) purposes" (2010, 14)

Teachers want to work in a safe environment. A school, due to great leadership, might be safe, but, if the surrounding area is not, those capable of finding positions in less depressed and safer neighborhoods will do so. Those who begin careers in blighted areas will often transfer out once they gain seniority.

"Teacher turnover hits high-poverty schools—where students already have the fewest resources—the hardest. Teachers are nearly twice as likely to exit high-poverty schools compared to the most affluent schools. With high annual turnover, children from low-income families are most likely to be taught by a novice teacher" (Redding 2018, para. 5).

On the one hand, Redding notes that a supportive school environment created by the principal can reduce turnover; on the other hand, many teachers assigned to high-poverty schools come from alternative programs and "often have less of an attachment to teaching as a long-term career as teachers prepared through traditional university-based programs. We show that 23 percent of traditionally prepared teachers leave teaching by the end of their third year compared to 45 percent of alternatively certified teachers" (2018, para. 12).

Let's put this altogether. The location of the school building affects the quality of the education offered because it impacts on the hiring and retention of teachers. A school in a low-crime, safe neighborhood, with local amenities and easy access to public transportation, will draw and maintain more traditionally certified teachers than schools in a high-crime area with few amenities and longer walks to public transportation.

We need more studies that directly ask teachers and principals about this location factor. It is probably more important than the poverty level of the students in the school. Districts can't change the locations of schools, and government is not providing programs to reduce poverty and help neighborhoods regenerate.

Suburban and especially rural schools have fewer location problems but have other issues. For example, older students often drive to school with all the incumbent hazards of possibly hundreds of inexperienced drivers congregating on one campus with elementary and middle school age students inattentively walking about as they text and tweet.

Statisticians who rate schools must consider the physical plant and location of the school when they create their rating formulas. They need to include the following areas, over which school leaders and teachers have little or no control:

- The negative effect of overcrowding overall in the school as a whole and in hall and classroom spaces in particular
- The difficulty of changing school design (or classroom capacity) to provide for teacher and parent centers and student computer/study rooms
- The budgetary strains caused by school design, which increase security costs and reduce instructional capability
- Antiquated or nonexistent facilities—electrical wiring, heating, science laboratories, technology, physical education spaces, athletic fields, music and art rooms, cafeterias, and auditoriums
- Because of school downsizing and shared spaces, inadequate grade-level and subject-area supervision and teacher evaluation
- The inequity of capital spending on schools located in areas of poverty
- The impact a blighted neighborhood can have on the recruitment and retention of teachers

We can be sure that these mathematical geniuses either will create an analytic that no one can understand or discount the impact of building design, maintenance, and location, issues over which pedagogues have no control.

Chapter Four

Parents

This chapter explores the impact of parents on student success. Before beginning school, children are the responsibility of their parents and extended family. What happens during this time is critical to the development of children and determines their learning readiness. Schools are expected to bring all students up to predetermined levels of competency regardless of the level and type of parenting during these critical formative years.

After entering kindergarten, children still spend the majority of their time outside of the school. Let's do the math. There are 8,760 hours in a year (365 x 24). Students are in school approximately 200 days for about seven hours a day, or 1,400 hours (200 x 7). If we optimistically assume that children spend eight hours a night sleeping, or 2,920 hours (365 x 8), then during the year a child spends 4,440 waking hours outside the school (8,760 − 1,400 − 2,920). Of the child's 5,840 waking hours, only 24% (1,400/5,840) is spent in school. The other 76% is spent with family, child caregivers, or peers.

Current statistical analyses evaluate the success of children and hence the success of teachers, supervisors, and schools on the basis of 24% of students' waking time. They downplay that, during the first four years of their lives, they weren't even in school. If we do the math on a child's first eighteen years of life, this means that of their 105,120 waking hours, only 19,600 are spent in school, or 18.6%.

We can critique this in many ways. Children may stay in school for co- or extracurricular activities. This is not instruction. They may stay for enrichment classes, but this is probably offset by less sleeping time and more waking hours at home or with peers. We can argue that at least one period (40 to 45 minutes per school day) is spent in the lunchroom with peers, not on instruction.

To round everything off, during their formative years, children spend at least 80% of their waking time with family, child caregivers, and peers, time not considered by the analytics used to evaluate schools. School districts themselves know how crucial this time is, hence, the current movement to have children begin school earlier through pre-K and 3–K programs that will give schools up to 24% of a child's waking time during their fourth and fifth years.

Teachers see the best and the worst of the parents of their students. They see children who come to school with signs of abuse or neglect. Some lack proper clothing; some are malnourished. Young children often tell their teachers details of their lives at home. Or a teacher can tell by a child's withdrawal into self that something is wrong. Older children write essays and compositions for English class and reveal much about their home and neighborhood life under the guise of fiction.

The majority of children have loving, caring parents and a positive home life. Teachers find that most of the parents they speak with show true concern for their children and, if there is a problem, want to know what they can do to help. This despite the often devastating effects of living in poverty. Sometimes, caring parents can be overly protective, but educators know how to counsel them.

Some very well-meaning parents cause difficulties not because of lack of caring but because they think they know more than the teacher or the principal and feel free to criticize the curriculum, pedagogy, or school administration. This relates to the diminishing respect and prestige of educators, which will be examined in Chapters 7 and 8. Making sure the school is transparent, keeping the school website up to date, and having ongoing communication with parents reduce the tensions such well-meaning parents may cause.

Elementary school principal Ms. Wren kept a computer file on the calls or visits from parents she personally handled. For each parent she had a file with the name of the child and their expected year of graduation, the name and preferred phone number and email of the parent, the date and reason for the call or visit, and the action taken or resolution reached.

At the end of June, she went through her file. Most parent files had one entry for a minor matter; however, there were thirty files with multiple entries. These thirty parents (out of a school population of 650) indicated that just under 5% of the students and parents were responsible for almost 90% of the issues Ms. Wren personally addressed. Some were those described above—the overprotective parents, the parents who felt they could run the school better themselves, and, sometimes, the parents who needed help controlling their own children.

These parents cared about the welfare of their children and came with problems or questions to work with the school to solve them. But the angriest parents came to complain about reports made about them to child welfare agencies.

The loving parents, the overprotective parents, even the I-know-more-than-you parents are not the ones educators remember. What is seared into most teachers' and school leaders' minds are the children who are victims and parents or caregivers who demonstrate little or no regard for their children's well-being.

Principal Rayne never forgot an incident that took place during her first year as a high school teacher during her first parent–teacher conference. Joel was an average student in her ninth-year English class. He almost never volunteered an answer. He tended to be self-effacing and shy, rarely interacting with other students. Ms. Rayne was trying to think of ways to have him come out of his shell.

On this evening, Joel arrived in the classroom with his father, whose first words were "How is my dummy doing?" His remarks deteriorated from there, despite Ms. Rayne's repeated attempts to relate all the positives about Joel, who was shrinking into himself as his father spoke. The next morning, she spoke with Joel's guidance counselor and reported the incident. The counselor told her that she was already trying to arrange an intervention, but the parents were uncooperative.

Twenty-four years later in another high school where she was now principal, Ms. Rayne was involved in a more violent parent–teacher conference incident. While a teacher was calmly explaining to a mother what her daughter needed to do to make up work to pass the class, the mother suddenly got up, went over to the child, and smacked her across the face. The teacher immediately stood up to protect the child, whereupon the mother grabbed the teacher by the throat. An AP walking by the classroom saw what was happening, restrained the mother, and had the teacher call school security.

Ms. Rayne called the police, who took the mother into custody; child services found shelter for the child. Shortly thereafter, she was placed in foster care.

A parent stormed past his secretary and angrily confronted middle school principal Mr. Joaquin in his conference room. She demanded to speak to him, her child's guidance counselor, and the assistant principal. Mr. Joaquin said he would call them (he also had his secretary call security). Once the counselor and AP were present, the parent pulled out a tape recorder and said she was taping everything. She then proceeded to rant about how terrible the school and its teachers were. It was clear from the parent's remarks that the counselor, after conferencing with the child's teachers, had called child services to report the parent for educational neglect because she had repeatedly not come to the school for conferences concerning her daughter's absences, lateness, poor academic performance, and behavioral issues.

The parent took the heavy cane she had with her and began to bang it on the table as she began to scream obscenities. At this point, security arrived and restrained her; the police were called, and the parent was escorted to a nearby station house. The parent was committed for psychological evaluation, and the child (and her sister) placed in foster care.

Jolene is a four-year-old. Her mother abandoned her in the hospital after giving birth. Jolene had to remain for several weeks because drugs had passed from her mother's bloodstream, making her addicted to heroin.

Through a friend who worked in child services, Ms. Beth and her partner, both teachers, sought to adopt Jolene after first having her as a foster child. Both were fingerprinted and underwent thorough background checks. They had to prove they had medical coverage. Child Services representatives checked their home to be sure it was a safe environment. Once Jolene was in their care, they were visited every month; during the visit, Jolene was interviewed separately so she could speak freely. The birth mother had signed away her rights, but Ms. Beth still had to make two court appearances before the adoption would be finalized.

Bringing children into this world is a natural process, and some would add an inherent even deity ordained right. It is an accepted fact that not everyone knows how to be a parent and raise children. That's why there are bookshelves of parenting books and myriads of parenting classes. That is why there are child welfare agencies. That is why there are foster homes.

It is also assumed that parents want to have children and look forward to raising them into adulthood. But some children are unplanned or "accidents." Some parents want to have a child to save an already shaky marriage. Many couples are totally unaware of the physical, psychological, and financial tolls of raising a child. The lack of legislated paid parental leave and the cost of day care are problems for all parents but especially for those already living in poverty.

Being a parent is a learn-on-the-job responsibility. Children do not come with an instruction manual, and, since all parents and children are different, no books or classes can possibly address individual uniqueness. From an educational point of view, there are at least eleven aspects of parenting that have a major impact on a child's school performance.

(1) Maturity of parents. In general—and everything discussed in this section is "in general"—the more mature the parents, the more successful they will be at rearing children. More maturity usually means more stability, more patience, and more time spent with the child.

(2) Stability of family. A child raised in a stable household, whether traditional, nontraditional or blended, benefits from consistent parenting and direction in the formative years and thereafter.

(3) Pre- and postnatal care. Expectant mothers who have appropriate pre- and postnatal care tend to have fewer complicated pregnancies, healthier babies, and fewer postpartum issues. With the continuing weakening of Obamacare, providing appropriate health care for expectant and postpartum mothers is becoming more costly. There are many families and single parents who neglect their own health simply because they cannot afford it.

(4) Access to books and reading. A household with age-appropriate books is a positive, assuming the adults spend time reading to children and discussing what was read.

(5) Limited access to all media. Not so long ago, this would have been written as limited television time and monitoring to ensure that programs watched had appropriate educational or recreational content. Now, it must include computers, tablets, and cell phones, making the task far more complex. Decades ago, Robert Fulghum's book *All I Need to Know I Learned in Kindergarten* was a best-seller among baby boomers. It stressed the importance of socialization skills. Mr. Rogers did the same in his syndicated TV program. The greatest threat to children learning these skills in the pre- and early school years is overuse of electronics taking time away from socializing with peers and adults.

(6) Greater access to playtime with other children. Once parents took children to a playground and allowed them to explore and play with other children under ever vigilant eyes. This is still possible, although many parents' not-so-vigilant eyes are now on their cell phones, rather than their children. More frequently, children have "play dates" where two or more parents arrange for their children to meet at a specific time and place. This is fine but limits the child's experience of others to a small circle of often ethnically and culturally similar friends. Children need to experience the larger world.

(7) Serving as positive role models. Parents must be role models and teach children how to interact socially with adults and peers. They need to teach their children responsibility, respect, and manners. In a world where adults are becoming more uncivil and enamored of social media, rather than face-to-face meetings, appropriate social interaction seems to be a lost art. How often do we see a family having dinner in a restaurant where both parents are on their cell phones while their children unsuccessfully try to speak with

them or are themselves engrossed in their tablets? One can only surmise that the same is true at home.

(8) Attendance at parent–teacher conferences and school events. Parents need to know the schools their children go to and meet teachers and supervisors. Almost all schools outreach to parents in multiple ways, from the kindergarten parent orientation, to "back-to-school" nights, parent–teacher conferences, award nights, student performances and ceremonies, and parent workshops on a variety of topics. The more events parents attend, the more they meet and get to know teachers and other school personnel. Likewise, timely responses to school communications indicate parent interest in the welfare of their children. Unfortunately, parents forced by circumstances to work multiple jobs may not be able to attend school events or respond to communications in a timely fashion.

Most schools have websites where information about the school is a keystroke away: school policies, the school calendar, a list of staff members and how to contact them, and upcoming school events. Some make use of programs that allow parents to check their children's attendance, homework, and academic progress. If a parent sees a potential problem, it can be addressed immediately. This is a benefit to parents with internet access but not for those whose income does not allow for this, roughly one quarter of households with school-age children (Editorial Board 2020).

(9) Support for the teacher and school. In times past, the teacher was always right. Today's grandparents can vividly recall coming home to tell their parents how a teacher yelled at them. Their parents responded, "Well, what did you do wrong?" before punishing them for not listening to the teacher. Today, the pendulum has swung 180 degrees the other way. Let a child say to a parent "the teacher told me my homework was poorly done," and the parent will be outside the principal's office complaining that the teacher hurt the child's feelings. Neither extreme is correct.

Sometimes, a teacher is wrong. Sometimes, in frustration, a teacher speaks out of turn. On very rare occasions, a teacher really doesn't belong in a classroom. But 99.9% of the time, teachers are doing their jobs, which includes admonishing poor behavior and critically appraising student work and performance. This is difficult in a world where children are praised as artists for their scribblings and told that everyone who competes in any type of event is a winner. It sounds so good and is so not the real world. Perhaps as parents become more versed in growth mindset ideology (through school workshops?), there will be greater understanding between parents and teachers.

(10) See to the health of their children: childhood vaccinations, regular medical and dental checkups, etc. CHIP (Children's Health Insurance Program) is the federal government's plan to make sure that all children have

access to inexpensive health care, but each state implements it differently. What is inexpensive to one person could be a day's food allowance or winter coat for another. This relates to #11 below.

(11) Income inequality and poverty. What parents earn, how many jobs they need to hold down, and their living locations and homes impact on the success of their children. Just as many aspects of a child's success are beyond the control of teachers and principals, so this is beyond the control of parents who must do whatever possible to provide for their families.

According to the *New York Times*, the education of the mother is also a critical factor. In 2016, the average age of a first-time mother was 26.3. The average age for a woman with a college degree was 30.3, and for one without a degree, was 23.8. This difference strongly affects the future prospects of the child and can further widen inequality (Bui and Cain Miller 2018).

All of the above impact on a child's social and academic readiness for school. Statisticians create complex analytics to define the impact teachers have on children. Perhaps they should do the same for parents, whose influence is greater than any one teacher's.

Not all our assumptions about a family's living in poverty are true. Sometimes, the research belies expectations. It might be assumed, for example, that childcare arrangements for children before they enter kindergarten would be less regular for those living in poverty. The US Census looked at childcare arrangements based on certain characteristics of the mother. There was little difference between those below the federal poverty line and those above, with two exceptions. Those living below the poverty line were more likely to have childcare provided by a "sibling or other relative," 20.7% to 9.0%, and were less likely to use day care or nursery preschool, 19.5% to 32.4% (Laughlin 2013, 3).

Sometimes, research proves that some beliefs are partially true. It is commonly believed that children of poverty miss more days of school than those living above the poverty line, leading to poorer academic performance. The difference is not as great as one would suspect. According to the Centers for Disease Control and Prevention (2013), 13.8 million school days were missed due to asthma. Nationwide, 49% of all children with asthma missed at least one day of school; 54.8% of children with asthma living below the poverty level missed at least one day of school. "At least one day" does not tell us how many in each category missed five or ten or more days.

On the other hand, we know that 14% of children living in poverty experience asthma, compared to 8% not living in poverty. Those in poverty are exposed to problems associated with high-density housing, such as mold, drafts, and even cigarette smoke from nearby apartments. They may also have difficulty accessing medications and going for medical appointments (MacKay 2016, 1).

Children living in poverty may also suffer from the effects of "food insecurity," a term frequently used during the COVID-19 crisis when millions lost their incomes as large segments of the nation shut down.

Food insecurity existed before the pandemic. The US Department of Agriculture reported that 11.1% of households were food insecure sometime during 2018. This affected over 37 million people, including 6 million children. Over half a million children had very low food security, meaning normal eating patterns were disrupted "and food intake was reduced at times during the year because they had insufficient money or other resources for food (Coleman-Jensen et al. 2019, 7–10). Not surprisingly, most food insecure households were low income (Coleman-Jensen et al. 2019, 15).

What are the results of food insecurity? The *Huffington Post* reports, "More than 12 million households are forced to eat unhealthy food because they can't afford better-quality groceries. They risk adverse health effects that can make their financial plight worse." In addition, "66 percent of households said they've had to choose between paying for food and paying for medicine or medical care. Thirty-one percent said they had to make that choice every month" (Stuart 2014).

According to the US Census, 17.5% of people under the age of 18 live in poverty—that's 12.8 million (Fontenot, Semega, and Kollar 2018, 14).

A single Mom worked two jobs. One day, she arrived home, made dinner, sat and read with her child, and then tucked her into bed. Once she was sure the child was asleep, she decided to soak in the tub to relax—and fell asleep. When she awoke an hour later, she checked on her child and found she was not in her bed or anywhere in the house. She frantically went through the building and then into the surrounding neighborhood. Two blocks away, she found that the police had located her child, wandering the streets. The mother was arrested for neglect and the child referred to child services. Fortunately, a wise family court judge, apprised of all the details, released the mother and had the child returned. Not all such stories end well.

Another single mom worked three jobs to provide for her children and pay the rent. Every day she was physically exhausted. On a frigid winter's evening, driving from one job to another, she saw an opportunity to get a short rest. She parked and fell asleep. There was no heat in the car. She froze to death.

These mothers, like so many other parents, try to do the best for their children. They must contend with substandard housing (even in public housing projects) and work multiple jobs just to make ends meet. They still need to worry whether the rent will be paid, their children will have winter coats, or they can put meals on the table. They may have to deal with upheaval as they are moved from one temporary housing location to another. At the same time they maintain a positive disposition and help their children lead as normal a life as possible.

They face more than the normal health issues from poor living conditions, poor nutrition, and the wear and tear of working multiple jobs. While medical coverage is available for most children and adults can apply for Medicaid, a parent may not have the time to wait hours on end in a clinic or office. Earning a living is the priority, and the loss of even a few hours' pay might mean no dinner for the day.

It is much worse for illegal immigrants, who fear contact with any government agency. Even when told it will not impact on their being able to stay in the US, many will not even try to take advantage of free health and social service programs.

Given all this, it is amazing how many poor children not only survive but thrive. For some, however, the world is a bleak place when their parents surrender to the effects of poverty and take out their frustrations on their children.

Few parents bring a child into this world planning to maltreat them, but poverty can be relentless. Families and single parents who cannot afford the bare essentials deal with survival issues on a daily basis. The studies show that poverty and child maltreatment go hand in hand.

Let's look at the data:

- "Children in low socioeconomic status households had significantly higher rates of maltreatment. . . . They experienced some type of maltreatment more than 5 times the rate of other children" (Sedlak et al. 2010, 12).
- The US has one of the worst records on child abuse among industrialized nations, losing between four and seven children every day to child abuse and neglect ("Child Abuse Statistics and Facts" 2014).
- It is estimated that 1,720 children died from abuse and neglect in 2017. It is estimated that between 50% and 60% of maltreatment fatalities are not recorded on death certificates (American Society for the Positive Care of Children 2018).
- In 2017, nearly 48% of maltreatment victims were three years old or under (American Society for the Positive Care of Children 2018).
- Child Protective Agencies screened 2.4 million referrals in all fifty-two reporting states. The majority were investigated. This represents a rate of 31.8 referrals for each 1,000 children ("Child Maltreatment 2017" 2019, 6).
- The majority of perpetrators of child maltreatment are parents, 77.6%, or other relatives, 6.3% ("Child Maltreatment 2017" 2019, 68).
- The majority of perpetrators of child maltreatment are white, just under 50% ("Child Maltreatment 2017" 2019, 67).

Pub.Med.com, the website for the National Library of Medicine, provides an abstract of an article that appeared in *Pediatrics*. The main conclusion reads as follows: "Higher income inequality across US counties was significantly associated with higher county-level rates of child maltreatment. The findings contribute to the growing literature linking greater income inequality to a range of poor health and well-being outcomes in infants and children" (Eckenrode et al. 2014).

So that we are clear about our terms, "child maltreatment" refers to neglect, physical abuse, and sexual abuse: 74.9% of the incidents involved neglect, 18.3% physical abuse, and 8.6% sexual abuse. Some incidents involve two or more of these categories ("Child Maltreatment 2017" 2019, 58).

Several sources provide reams of additional information and statistics on child maltreatment in the United States. The data cited here concentrates on socioeconomic issues. Other factors impacting on child maltreatment include family structure, family living arrangements, and family size. Drug and alcohol abuse, as well as mental illness, are also involved.

While there is a definite correlation between poverty and child abuse/neglect (Sedlak et al. 2010, 14), the majority of poor parents provide as best they can for their children. School leaders and teachers know that parents from all income levels may be guilty of child neglect or abuse. One form, psychological abuse (described in the previously cited anecdote about student Joel), is not measured by the statistics.

What can they learn from the reports and studies?

- Because so many reports and studies are done by government agencies, federal, state, and local politicians are aware of the relationship between poverty, income inequality, and child maltreatment.
- Nearly half of all maltreatment occurs in the first three years of a child's life, before they enter the educational system, before a teacher can see and report a problem.
- If 31.8 referrals per 1,000 children tend to be the yearly norm, the chances are that in any class of thirty, at least one child is a victim of maltreatment. This is a low estimate, as the child may have been maltreated in a past year and incidents of maltreatment are underreported. A more realistic estimate would be between two and four in a class of thirty.
- A parent is the perpetrator in nearly eight out of ten incidents of maltreatment.
- Poverty and income inequality are at the center of maltreatment, not race or ethnicity.

There are no coordinated programs to reduce poverty or income inequality. Nor are there national programs to address paid parental leave and childcare needs. While there is a program for children's health, there is little for pre- and postnatal maternity care.

The COVID-19 pandemic shone a light on the chasm between the haves and have-nots of our country: those who could leave infected areas for their vacation homes and those who had to remain in substandard housing; those who work in the service industries (for minimum wages) losing their jobs and those who were able to work from home and collect salaries; those who face food insecurity and eviction and those whose main worry is finding hand sanitizer and toilet paper; those with untreated serious illnesses and poor health care access and those with good health insurance coverage who have preexisting conditions under control; those who have little or no computer hardware and internet access and those who have multiple computers and easy access; those who experience the injustice of the policing and the legal systems and those who assume both are fair and equitable.

In the spring of 2020, our nation witnessed what happens when a long history of collective injustice becomes focused by one egregious act of violence and combines with the poverty and income inequality rampant in our country exacerbated by the job losses and deprivations of the pandemic lockdown. As the protests evolved, the demands for justice added demands for a redistribution of resources to address the social needs of families and children. Will these protests lead to programs that address injustice, poverty, income inequality, and the needs of all children? Or will our political leaders assume the turmoil will dissipate and just go back to business as usual?

Principals and teachers have no control over the first three to five years of a child's life, the most formative years. They have no control over what happens to a child the 80% of the time a child is not in school. They have no control over the grinding effects of poverty on children, from unsafe and inadequate housing, to lack of parental interactions, poor nutrition, poor access to health care, and the injustices of the legal system.

Schools do not create societal ills. Daily, however, they must work with parents and children who grapple with them. In most cases, they work together to do the best for children. In some cases, they become mandatory reporters of child neglect and abuse. In some cases, they must try to help children who are traumatized. In the next chapter, we will look further into the impact on poverty on children and its implications for schools and teachers.

Chapter Five

Students

"Kids are kids" is an old adage—times may change, but children are the same, generation after generation. Not anymore.

Over the past fifteen years, childhood has fundamentally changed so rapidly that parenting, society, and pedagogy have not kept pace. There are at least three causes for these changes: the loss of a sense of responsibility (discussed in the previous chapter), communication and information technology, and the psychological trauma of poverty exacerbated by the widening gap between rich and poor.

In this chapter, we will look at the last two changes and a significant problem: the very small percentage of children, unaffected by positive interventions, such as as PBIS or restorative justice, who prey on their classmates, disrupt instruction, and engage in unlawful activities.

Mr. Joaquin is an AP at a middle school. The school has a rule: if a student uses a cell phone during class, the phone will be confiscated until the parent comes to the school to retrieve it. On this particular Monday, Jill was caught texting during a lesson. The teacher called Mr. Joaquin, who brought Jill to his office, gave her a receipt for the cell phone, and then locked it in his secure cabinet. The student began to cry.

He called Jill's home and spoke to her father. He was very glad the school had confiscated the phone and told Mr. Joaquin that, to teach his daughter a lesson, he would not come to the school to pick it up until Friday. When Jill was told this, she threw a tantrum, crying and screaming; Mr. Joaquin called her guidance counselor (fortunately, in the next office), but even she could not calm Jill, who retreated into a semicatatonic state.

Mr. Joaquin called home again and explained the situation. Jill's father came to school and took her home. He left the phone locked in Mr. Joaquin's cabinet.

Adults wring their hands and wag their heads when talking about the younger generation and wonder how the world will survive when today's children become adults. Many of today's senior citizens recall how their parents felt that television, later coupled with rock and roll, would be the end of civilization. Today, the fear for the future is greater due to the breakneck pace of technological change.

Alexander Graham Bell invented the landline telephone in 1876. By the mid-20th century, it was the major means of communication for most Americans. Fifty years later, a mere 17% of users felt they could not part with their landlines (Tsukayama 2014). Today, this percentage is probably much lower, but the old Bell telephone had a good hundred year run.

Commercial radio came into its own in the early 20th century and was the main source of information for Americans during World War II. In the late 1940s, network television began to expand exponentially and was the major news source during the Cold War and Vietnam. Network TV still exists today but with viewership diminished by cable and internet companies. More and more Americans rely on the internet (and some very questionable sources) for information.

As the role of network television declined, communication and information technology kicked into high gear. Personal computers came into their own in the early 1980s and laptops and early cell phones in the 1990s. Today, the number of cell phones in the US significantly exceeds the population. The 2000s saw the explosion of social media: Facebook, Twitter, LinkedIn, YouTube, WhatsApp, Pinterest, and Instagram. The Apple App Store opened in 2008. Cell phones have moved from 1G to 5G. The past forty years have seen a total upheaval in communication and information technology.

Our students are the children of this communication/information revolution. They grew up with tablets and were babysat by their parents' cell phones. They are both the beneficiaries and victims of technology.

Technology has benefits. It brings the world together. It connects families in different parts of the country or world. It provides access to a wide range of materials for study and research. It has taken the tedium out of creating and editing documents and writing books.

So much about technology is good that it is easy for adults, let alone children, to forget its insidious side. Every time a user visits a website, information is stored and data mined, invading the privacy of the user and often others on their contact list. Inappropriate searches or postings never go away and, despite safeguards, are accessible by those the user might want excluded. Emails or tweets today could affect college admission or even future job prospects. No longer are the indiscretions of youth forgotten or sealed by the courts—the mistakes of childhood and adolescence are part of a permanent electronic record.

The very design of technology—the sounds and colors—are addictive to keep users enthralled. Students who should be interacting with peers face-to-face or even with an old-fashioned telephone call are texting, frequently with the first and often inappropriate word, picture, or emoji that comes to mind. Consequences that would be obvious face-to-face are lost under the veil of technology. Children who should be sleeping are staying up late into the night gaming or texting or posting.

It gets worse. Part of the educational process is learning to be open-minded and logical, to understand one's own beliefs but respect the beliefs of others, and to be able to engage in honest conversation with those with whom one disagrees without the use of insults or personal attacks. Such open dialogue reduces negativism, so important when dealing with impressionable youth.

Technology is a threat to serious, intellectual discourse. Erroneous ideas and extreme views that in the past would have isolated an individual, find credence and power with like-minded, misguided individuals through social media. Children (and adults) can find validation if they think the world is flat, if they feel measles vaccinations cause autism, or if they agree with Adolf Hitler. Instead of intelligent debate and an openness to the ideas of others, there is a hardening of stance and subscription only to websites in agreement with one's views. Instead of understanding, there is intolerance. This is the antithesis of education in a democratic society that "promotes the general welfare."

The list of negatives goes on. Cell phones and internet sites reduce attention spans as information is reduced to fifty-character tweets, catchy sound bites, and graphic images. The loss of face-to-face interactions makes children socially inept. Technology use encourages sedentary activity, increasing childhood obesity and diabetes. At least parental controls keep children away from harmful sites. Or do they? Search "children overriding parental controls," and you will find links such as:

- 3 Ways to bypass parental controls on a Mac (wikihow.com)
- How to get around parental controls on the internet (wikihow.com)
- How teens bypass parental controls like open DNS-Net Sanity (netsanity.net)
- Child account/parent control for Windows 10 has a hole (answers.microsoft.com)
- How well can kids get past parental control software (abcnews.go.com)

Under the Children's Internet Protection Act (CIPA), public schools and libraries that receive federal funds for internet access must install blocking software on computers that will be used by anyone under seventeen. Aside from concerns raised by the ACLU and the fact that some filters make it impossible for students to conduct legitimate research, you also have to wonder how many children can override these controls and access school websites, altering everything from schedules to grades.

How can we protect and educate children in this brave new world? Schools and teachers can have some impact, but they need help. Remember, children spend 80% of their waking hours with parents and peers.

- Schools can provide workshops for parents on how to limit and monitor the tech time of their children, but this is ineffective if parents do not attend or do not implement the ideas presented. At-home monitoring must be constant and consistent since children are adept at overriding controls.
- Schools can and should put limits on tech use, particularly tablets and cell phones. They should be prohibited with two exceptions: first, when needed for the child to contact a parent in an emergency (under the direction of a school authority), and second, when a teacher directs their use for an educational purpose. A student using a device for any other reason should have the device confiscated until a parent comes to the school to retrieve it.
- Schools need to educate students on tech use: how to protect their privacy, how to use it to their benefit, what material is inappropriate. This will require funding to train teachers (who themselves may be unaware of much of this). Fordham University's Center on Law and Information Policy (CLIP) provides free and open-source materials for educators, including a full set of lesson plans that can be adapted for different age groups. There is an online training manual for teachers and information for parents, school leaders, and districts: https://www.fordham.edu/info/24071/privacy_education.

We cannot talk about technology without discussing bullying. In 2013, 22% of students reported being bullied, a reduction from 30% in 2007 (Musu-Gillette et al. 2015), but still more than one in five children.

Bullying is nothing new. When one looks at novels dealing with school life over the past 200 years, one finds that bullies are everywhere. They are part of the lore of the English public school—even up to the popular Harry Potter series, where we find that Harry's beloved father bullied Snape when they were students at Hogwarts. Look at popular movies, from *The Karate Kid*; to *Back to the Future*; to *Scent of a Woman*; and to *Going My Way*, where the gang leader bullies underlings, under the approving eyes of Father O'Malley.

Citing history doesn't condone bullying; it only verifies it is not a new phenomenon. In literature and the movies, however, bullying isn't reported to the teacher—that would be snitching. The one bullied learns how to confront the bully, usually finding the strength to fight back, such as Ralphie in *A Christmas Story*.

Giving the bully a black eye would not be acceptable today. In our more civilized world, Ralphie would have reported the bully to the teacher or principal who would have brought all parties to the table to resolve their conflicts. The school would create an individualized support plan for the bully, who would be monitored to ensure that improper behavior did not recur. Ralphie would also receive counseling for trauma and provided with strategies to deal with future incidents of bullying.

Even as we dismiss these literary and cinematic examples as condoning inappropriate responses and unlikely fantasy (the bully always loses), there is a kernel of truth we may have minimized in our efforts to eradicate bullying: part of growing up is learning how to deal with the bullies of this world and to recognize what bullying is and is not. A child saying she doesn't like another's sneakers is not bullying. Neither is a coach telling a team member that he will be benched for not performing up to par. Neither is a teacher telling a student that surreptitious texting is unacceptable. We need to ask ourselves, "Are we preparing our students for the world after school?"

In life after school, where does legitimate use of power end and bullying begin? Will the graduates of our schools know the difference? What is the difference between a boss who is demanding and expecting a high level of performance from one who is a bully? What would a graduate of our restorative justice system say to a supervisor who has just told them that the video presentation submitted was "garbage" and needed to be redone? Are we, as educators, overdefining bullying and making clear that bullying is not legitimate criticism or merely the statement of an opinion?

There are no easy answers. In addition to providing students with mechanisms to deal with bullies and a way to report bullying when these fail, we need to alert them to what may lie in the future. Perhaps, with our older students, we need to explain the realities of the world they will be going into where reporting what they feel is bullying could cost them their jobs, especially in a society where bullying at the highest levels of political power is condoned by more than one third of the voting population.

Face-to-face bullying has merged with modern technology into cyberbullying. This is the most insidious aspect of technology for today's students. Schools can lay down rules for physical bullying seen on campus. Fear of being caught on camera or reported can hold bullies in check. But what happens when there is no fear of repercussions in the anonymity of the internet?

Schools are told they need to address this issue even if the cyberbullying occurs off-campus on the students' own cell phones or computers. This is impractical and impossible unless the schools can require what would be unacceptable to students and their parents: (1) close all social media accounts and never go on social media again and (2) change cell phone numbers and give them only to family members; all others can call on the home landline (if the home has one). This would put an end to cyberbullying and to many other negative aspects of technology. It will never happen.

Educators cannot control what goes on during the 80% of waking time students are not in school. The older the child gets, the greater the percentage of this time is spent with peers, much of it through electronic devices. And some of these peers (or faux peers) are not part of their school or neighborhood coteries but "internet friends."

Any attempt to legislate what students do outside the school is unenforceable and doomed to failure. The role of the school is to educate—parents, students, and staff. In the case of cyberbullying, the best advice is reporting incidents to the police. Schools simply do not have the time, personnel, expertise, equipment, and subpoena power available to law enforcement authorities.

Chapter 4 documented that 17.5% of American children—12.8 million—live in poverty and that income inequality leads to higher rates of child maltreatment. We can add poor nutrition, inadequate housing, and sometimes living in dangerous or violent neighborhoods. And homelessness. Such conditions are also the breeding grounds for substance abuse and gangs. "Based on a calculation using the most recent data from the U.S. Department of Education and the 2013 U.S. Census, 2.5 million children in America—one in every 30 children—go to sleep without a home of their own each year" (Bassuk et al. 2014, 6).

Poverty has a direct negative impact on a child's education as was discovered when schools closed during the COVID-19 pandemic. "Even before the shutdown, an estimated 12 million children were having difficulty completing routine assignments—not to mention writing research papers—because they lacked the home internet access that better-off classmates take for granted" (Editorial Board 2020).

Many school districts scrambled to provide students with the technology needed for distance learning. "New York City, which has an estimated 300,000 students who lack internet-connected devices, is one of several districts rushing to acquire such devices" (Editorial Board 2020).

The problem was worse for students living in rural areas. "In Fairfield County, South Carolina, 51% of households have no broadband internet access, according to an Associated Press analysis of census data. Nationwide, an estimated 18% of U.S. students do not have home access to broadband internet." In short, "The pandemic that launched a massive, unplanned experiment with distance learning has created extraordinary hurdles for schoolchildren left behind by the digital divide" (Associated Press 2020).

Districts large and small scrambled to help students. This begs the question: What were districts doing to help these children before the pandemic—and what will they do afterward?

The abstract of a study published in *JAMA: Pediatrics* says the following:

> Data collected by the National Center for Education Statistics show that 51% of students across US public schools were from low-income families in 2013. Socioeconomic disparities in school readiness and academic performance are well documented. Children living in poverty have lower scores on standardized tests of academic achievement, poorer grades in school, and lower educational attainment. These patterns persist into adulthood, ultimately contributing to low wages and income. Moreover, increased exposure to poverty in childhood is tied to greater deficits in these domains. (Hair et al. 2015)

The same study concludes the following:

> Our work suggests that specific brain structures tied to processes critical for learning and educational functioning (eg, sustained attention, planning, and cognitive flexibility) are vulnerable to the environmental circumstances of poverty, such as stress, limited stimulation, and nutrition. If so, it would appear that children's potential for academic success is being reduced at young ages by these circumstances. Such understanding should lead to public policy initiatives aimed at improving and decreasing disparities in human capital. (Hair et al. 2015)

In a policy paper for the National Education Association, Ernest Izard notes the following:

> The first three years of life are critical. A child in its first three years needs to be attuned. That means they need to be talked to, played with, appropriately touched, and held. They need to be responded to when they have a biological need of hunger, thirst, elimination, or comfort. They also need to experience a gradual, safe separation from caregivers so that they do not experience an attachment disorder later. The children who are played with, read to, and experience quality music have brains that develop exponentially in their capacity for future learning. Nothing can substitute for face-to-face, eye-to-eye, and meaningful skin-to-skin moments. Without those necessary components of childrearing, a child may grow up to display mental and social challenges. (2016, 17–18)

Even if every school district instituted 3–K and pre-K programs, no child would be in school during these first three crucial years of their lives.

In her *Newsweek* article, Ericka Hayasaki (2016) surveys and summarizes several medical and scientific studies: "Early results show a troubling trend: Kids who grow up with higher levels of violence as a backdrop to their lives, based on MRI scans, have weaker real-time neural connections and interaction in parts of the brain involved in awareness, judgment, and ethical and emotional processing."

She goes on to note that impoverished children have less gray matter, which could affect memory, decision-making, problem solving, impulse control, judgment, and social emotional behavior as well as language, visual and auditory processing, and self-awareness. She concludes, "Working together, these brain areas are crucial for following instructions, paying attention and overall learning—some of the keys to academic success" (Hayasaki 2016).

The article defines the aspects of poverty that impact children: unsafe, dilapidated buildings; implicit racial bias; malnutrition; and underfunded schools in poor communities. It documents that the very skills a child needs for success in school and life are negatively affected.

This gets worse when we add the problems of substance abuse and gang affiliation and influence.

The US Department of Health and Human Services (n.d.) provides us with disturbing data, based on national surveys of children from 2017:

- Sixteen percent of high school students reported that they drank alcohol (other than a few sips) for the first time before they were thirteen years of age.
- Thirteen percent of high school students reported they had four or more alcoholic drinks in a row within a couple of hours on at least one day during the thirty days before the survey.
- Thirty-six percent of high school students reported they used marijuana one or more times.
- Five percent of high school students reported using some form of cocaine in their lifetime.
- Six percent of high school students reported they sniffed glue, breathed the contents of aerosol spray cans, or inhaled paints or sprays to get high, one or more times in their lifetime.
- Four percent of adolescents twelve to seventeen reported using pain relievers during the past year, not directed by a doctor.

DoSomething.org (2014) provides additional facts about teens and drug use:

- More teens die from prescription drugs than heroin/cocaine combined.
- In 2013, more high school seniors regularly used marijuana than cigarettes, as 22.7% smoked pot in the past month, compared to 16.3% who smoked cigarettes.

- The US represents 5% of the world's population and 75% of prescription drugs taken. Sixty percent of teens who abuse prescription drugs get them free from friends and relatives.
- By the eighth grade, 28% of adolescents have consumed alcohol, 15% have smoked cigarettes, and 16.5% have used marijuana.
- Of high school seniors, 6.5% smoke pot daily, up from 5.1% five years ago.

How does substance abuse impact on school performance? "Teens who smoke, drink alcohol, binge drink or use marijuana or other drugs are more likely than non-users to drop out of school and less likely than non-users to graduate from high school, attend college or obtain a college degree. One study found that nearly one-third of school dropouts indicate that their use of alcohol or other drugs was an important contributor in their decision to leave school" (Just Think Twice n.d.). Drug use can affect brain development and functioning by interfering with neurotransmitters, affecting the way the brain processes and retains information and how a child thinks, learns, remembers, focuses and concentrates.

The same learning and socialization problems caused by the trauma of poverty are exacerbated by substance abuse, making the issues faced by teachers and school leaders even more severe.

This trauma may also result in gang affiliation: "the majority of students who join gangs do so for protection. Gangs are most common in low-income communities, where going to school can be just as dangerous as walking alone down the street at night" (Calm Every Storm Crises Consultant Group. n.d.).

Even though gang activity in schools has diminished significantly in recent years, gangs maintain a presence. A survey of students twelve to eighteen years old revealed that 9% felt that gangs were present in their schools. This cut across localities with 11% of urban school students, 8% of suburban students, and 7% of rural students reporting a gang presence. Gang presence was reported in middle schools, with 5% of students reporting a gang presence in sixth and seventh grades and 7% in eighth grade (Musu et al. 2019).

Poverty and income inequality leading to blighted and unsafe neighborhoods are breeding grounds for gangs where children (and adults) feel a need for security and protection. This is exacerbated by mistrust, often founded, in the legal system and police forces charged with protecting them. "Black adults are about five times as likely as whites to say they've been unfairly stopped by police because of their race or ethnicity (44% vs. 9%)." This is especially true of black males, 59% (DeSilver, Lipka, and Fahmy 2020). Latinos and other recent immigrants, especially in recent years, live with the fear of deportation and so eschew all government entanglements, including law enforcement.

If you have no trust in the legal and policing systems, gangs provide the protection and security needed at the cost of engaging in illegal activities, which could lead to incarceration or premature death. When gangs have a presence on campus, school rules are often flouted and school authority diminished; criminal activities and bullying increase; and more students experience fear.

Not all poor children experience the same psychological and emotional issues. Many have parents who shield them from the violence of their neighborhoods. Many develop positive relationships with parents, teachers, and other adults "who make them feel secure and teach them coping mechanisms" (Hayasaki 2016). We know from the previous chapter, however, that some parents, themselves victims of poverty, do not provide help and security for their children.

Modern neuroscience tells us that the brain can change continually over our lifetimes. This is called neuroplasticity and has important implications for children who face the adversities of poverty in childhood. In short, there are strategies that governments, parents, and teachers can use to repair *some* of the damage of early and later childhood because the brain is continually evolving.

In his NEA booklet, Izard provides a list of actionable strategies teachers can use: build positive, enriching relationships (with children); create a safe atmosphere for learning; give students a sense of control; use a calm voice to teach; teach emotional skills; work with children who act out; work with withdrawn students; build short-term working memory; use expressive writing; teach reading skills; build students' vocabulary; teach self-regulation; teach empathy; provide meaningful touch (a problematic strategy in today's world); teach hope; and listen to the students' stories (Izard 2016, 25–33). Such strategies necessitate time for significant one-on-one teacher interaction, rarely possible in classrooms with twenty-five or more students.

Throughout his booklet, Izard lists the difficulties schools, teachers, and principals face in trying to help children of poverty and trauma, particularly schools located in low socioeconomic areas. He makes one comment that will give pause to today's educators: *"Schools are also at risk when they focus on less than a comprehensive approach to education, focusing solely on a curriculum and assessments that measure the attempts to teach to it"* (Izard 2016, 13–14).

Hayasaki notes that Congress, local governments, school boards, and the judicial system need to rethink social programs and policies for poor communities. The focus needs to be the first five years of a child's life and include help for parents. Schools can also help by teaching children of poverty coping mechanisms to protect their developing brains (Hayasaki 2016).

As a result of protests over police brutality and unequal policing policies, there is a movement to redistribute some of the funding for police departments to social service programs, especially to those that impact on the welfare of children. It is yet to be seen if this will happen.

To provide a contrast, let's once again look at Finland, a country with low poverty and income inequality rates and a government that understands that the social fabric of the country is critical to a child's educational growth. In Finland, "It is almost unheard of for a child to show up hungry or homeless. Finland provides three years of maternity leave and subsidized day care to parents. . . . In addition, the state subsidizes parents, paying them around 150 euros every month for every child until he or she turns 17." Also, "Schools provide food, medical care, counseling, and even taxi service if needed. Student health care is free" (Hancock 2011, 97).

When it comes to poverty, income inequality, and lack of parental and early childhood support, the US falls far short. Schools, teachers, and principals have no control over this nor over the first three years of a child's life. Their long-term effects have a serious negative impact on the ability of children to learn in school and on their future prospects as adults. Some will become children unaffected by positive behavioral interventions.

"Round up the usual suspects" takes on new meaning in a school environment. Ms. Rayne had been a dean and intervention specialist before becoming an assistant principal at a West Coast high school. One of her duties was to oversee school security. It took her only a few weeks to determine that over 90% of the incidents involved the same thirty or so students, about 2% of the 1,600 in the school.

Included in this 2% were almost all of the cases of bullying, fighting, theft, and serious classroom disruptions. Most of the other students feared this group of thirty, some of whom where known gang members; a few wanted to be like them and were hangers-on to their doings. Ms. Rayne knew that without immediate intervention this small percentage of students could grow and create chaos.

A review of their records showed that their disruptive behavior was not new. In middle school, they had engaged in the same negative activities. They had been referred to counselors, taken part in restorative justice sessions, or been referred to positive intervention programs. They had been suspended to the extent permitted by district regulations. Their behavior had not changed.

In high school, the same interventions were tried and failed. Ms. Rayne added a new tactic. Any student who committed an infraction would be in-

house suspended and remain there until a parent came to the school for a conference. In-house suspension placed the students in an isolated room where their classwork, assignments, and lunches were brought to them. A teacher supervised and assisted with any schoolwork-related questions that arose.

The students hated being away from their peers. The one-time offenders and then the hangers-on stopped being disruptive. But, with few exceptions, the 2% remained unfazed, returning to the in-house suspension room shortly after their parents came to the school. Eventually, most parents got tired of being called out of work to come to the school; many sought transfers for their children. Some students stopped coming to school.

Ms. Rayne knew this was a no-win situation, but it did reduce the number of serious infractions, lessened the fear of children, and made the school safer for students and staff. Some of the 2% were taken under the personal wing of individual assistant principals, teachers, and even Ms. Rayne herself. They tracked their charges daily and made frequent calls home to update their parents. This personal investment of time and effort helped a few to change their ways and eventually graduate—just a few.

Here is some data culled from *Indicators of School Crime and Safety: 2018*:

- "From 1992-2017, school victimization rates and rates of specific crimes (i.e., theft, violent victimization and serious victimization declined for students 12-18 both at school and away from school" (Musu et al. 2019, iv). Musu talks about increased safety measures, as greater use of cameras, more schools having written codes of conduct, improved visitor sign-in procedures, and increased hallway supervision by teachers and other adults. While violence prevention programs and positive disciplinary measures are not mentioned, one would hope they contributed to this decline. Nonetheless, the actual numbers are disturbing.
- "In 2017, students 12 to 18 experienced about 827,000 total victimizations (theft, nonfatal violent victimizations) at school and 503,800 victimizations away from school. These figures represent 33 victimizations per 1000 students at school, compared to 20 victimizations per 1000 students away from school" (Musu et al. 2019, iii).
- "In 2017, about 6% of students in grades 9-12 reported being threatened or injured with a weapon while on school property during the previous 12 months" (Musu et al. 2019, 41).
- "In 2017, 4% of students in grades 9-12 reported carrying a weapon on school property at least one day during the previous 30 days" (Musu et al. 2019, iii).

Positive intervention programs are making schools safer for students. They are helping children learn how to resolve conflicts without violence, giving them strategies they can use throughout their lives. And yet, as the statistics above make clear, thousands of students are still being victimized (and these figures do *not* include elementary and middle school–age children).

Ninety-eight percent of students will follow most of the rules most of the time. Of course, they will test the system; engage in childish behavior; take part in pranks; and, sometimes, in dealing with the many pressures of growing up, talk back to teachers, act sullenly, refuse to participate, or act out. Experienced teachers understand this and can take care of such matters. If a few students stretch things too far, there are deans, counselors, assistant principals, department chairs, and the principal for support. Schools have ladders of discipline in place that can almost always resolve the issues with the majority of these students.

Modern brain research, mentioned earlier, has helped educators better understand how positive interventions can help all students succeed. We know about brain elasticity and the brain's ability to continue to learn and grow, even if there was past trauma or other issues. Growth Mindset theory seems to have provided educators with new and effective tools to help students. All of this has positive application to most students.

But what about the few not affected? Even in this era of positive interventions, a small percentage continues to flaunt rules and victimize other students. What might prevent this? Educational interventions with much smaller classes and specially trained teachers. Additional support systems, including interventions by medical professionals, psychologists, and social workers. School budgets are designed to educate all the children. Schools cannot devote the money needed to pay for these interventions without major negative impact on the educational programs of all students.

The issues and problems described earlier in this book describe the reasons a small percentage of children do not respond to ordinary school interventions the same way as the majority of children do: poor parenting, the trauma of poverty, overall societal inequities, peer influence (especially from gangs), and substance abuse. Whatever the reasons, these few students cause almost all the serious disciplinary problems for teachers and school leaders.

In our age of supportiveness, the educational "rules of engagement" bend over backward to help individual students. "Discipline" has become a dirty word. Before any serious discipline can be enforced, interventions must be initiated, again and again. There are limits to how many times and for how long a child can be suspended. In the meantime, the majority of students have their educations disrupted, and many find themselves prey to the small percentage of their classmates who flaunt rules.

PBIS and restorative justice have reduced incidents and helped students who may have gone down the wrong path become productive members of the school community. (Lest we forget, however, these are not new but better thought-out and more formal manifestations of student courts, peer intervention, and staff-directed supports.) Let's take a moment to look more closely at PBIS interventions.

"What Is PBIS?" (PBIS Rewards n.d.) provides a pyramid to show "tiers of intervention." Eighty percent of students are in Tier 1 and require no intervention beyond the measures the school has taken to create a "positive matrix outlining the positive behaviors that they wish to establish school wide."

Ten to 15% fall into Tier 2. These students demonstrate at-risk behaviors. The intervention focuses "on specific groups of students and the underlying issues that may be causing the behavior," which may be social, emotional, or academic.

Roughly 5% of students do not respond to Tier 1 or 2 interventions. They exhibit "high-risk behavior" and may require an individualized plan implemented by a team of school personnel.

It is easy to see that the majority of the school's intervention resources are concentrated on 5% of the students. This is not a new phenomenon, and neither is the concept behind PBIS.

In well-organized schools before the positive intervention era, "troubled" students were often referred to school deans for disciplinary action; if they detected certain patterns, students were referred to counselors for ongoing intervention. When needed, counselors involved the assistant principals and individual teachers as an informal team to assist students. Sometimes, program changes were made to place students with teachers more adept at working with them. When necessary, counselors reached out to community social service resources for further support for the students and their families.

PBIS has taken this informal system and made it formal, requiring a written plan to assist each Tier 3 student. It is more organized but also more time consuming so that even more of the school's intervention resources are directed to the 5%. More teacher time is required. While most teachers do not object to informal meetings, they may find formal, lengthy meetings are taking time away from their classroom preparation or parent contact for their other students. Teachers' days are already filled with required professional development, curriculum meetings, planning sessions, and grade and subject meetings. We will explore how teachers are reacting to these greater time demands in Chapter 7.

There are two problems with PBIS-type interventions. First, as noted, limited resources are concentrated on 5% of the student body, leaving less for the other 95%, particularly the 10 to 15% in Tier 2. Second, these resources may not yield the results desired.

Let's look at a middle or high school with 1,000 students. Much of the intervention resources would be directed to about fifty students. This could mean an additional guidance counselor and/or social worker and overtime pay for teachers to remain after school for intervention conferences.

The cost? Up to two teaching positions or ten classes that could have benefited far more students—a study skills class for all sixth or ninth graders, enrichment programs for the gifted and talented (the often neglected special need students), an after-school intramural sports program, or an expanded art or music program. In a world of limited school funding, principals face tough decisions. In the current world of statistical ratings, the question on most principals' minds is "How can I use my limited funds to ensure the best results for the majority of my students?"

The answer may not be support for Tier 3 students if it detracts from the educations of Tier 1 and especially Tier 2 students. Let's look at what principal Rayne did several years ago.

High school principal Rayne knew that the district was looking at her five-year graduation rate as the prime statistical rating measure for her school and herself. She did an in-depth study of students who graduated within the past three years. She found that while almost all of her Tier 1 students graduated in five years, few of her Tier 3 students did. Many dropped out or were discharged as "overage" despite interventions. Her Tier 2 group was split, with about half graduating in five years. She decided to devote significant resources to her current juniors and seniors designated as Tier 2. She did not ignore the Tier 3s but reduced their support. The result? After two years, far more of her Tier 2 students graduated on time, bringing her five-year graduation rate to 90%. There was no change in the graduation rate of her Tier 3 students.

Ms. Rayne was getting more bang for her buck. She directed funds so that more students would graduate. In today's world of disaggregated data, she might have to direct funds differently, sacrificing students in Tier 2 to provide more support for those in Tier 3—helping fewer students and lowering the overall graduation rate. In a utopian world, districts would fully fund the support suggested for Tier 3 students, eliminating the need for the tough decision. It will never happen.

PBIS and similar programs have replaced traditional disciplinary measures to keep the school and its students safe. What happens to the Tier 3 students who do not respond to the individualized interventions and still engage in high-risk behaviors, dangerous for themselves and others, disrupting the education of the rest of the students in the school? If the interventions succeed for 60% of the Tier 3 students, this leaves 2% of the student population unaffected and for whom there are little or no traditional disciplinary consequences available.

A democratic society protects the rights of the individual but must also promote the common welfare. The latter seems to have been forgotten. When a small number of students, whether due to emotional or psychological problems or poor or abusive parenting or the trauma of growing up in poverty, disrupt the school and do not respond to any other methods, there must be some way of removing them from contact with other students.

Parents and teachers understand this. "Frustration in the Schools: Teachers Speak Out on Pay, Funding, and Feeling Valued" comments on the results of a poll included in the September 2019 issue of *Kappan* (K1–K23) (Kappaonline.org 2019). According to this poll, in 1969, 45% of K–12 parents felt that school discipline was not strict enough. This jumped to 51% in 2019. Seventy-four percent of K–12 parents and 71% of public school teachers support "zero tolerance." But they are unclear how to achieve zero tolerance with only 48% of parents and 43% of teachers supporting "automatic suspension/expulsion if a student accidentally brings a folding knife to school." This begs the question of how a weapon is "accidentally" brought to school.

Two percent in a school of 1,000—twenty students—is enough of a disruptive force to destroy the culture of a school. They will bring borderline Tier 2 students into their fold, expand their base, prey on other children, and create an atmosphere of fear. What does a school do when Tier 3 interventions fail or parents neglect to participate in conferences?

A challenge for today's school leaders is to ensure the safety of all students and staff at a time when it is deemed reactionary to discipline and suspend disruptive children. They have to try to do this in the 20% of the time that they have the students in school. Is this possible? Probably with varying degrees of success, but only with a massive reallocation of instructional funds for specialized guidance counselors, social workers, teachers, and security personnel to deal specifically with the 2%, reducing programs and services for the majority of students. No one is providing teachers and school leaders with a successful method of rehabilitating the small minority without impacting on the educational programs of all students.

The politicians will look at these numbers and say it proves that the schools are failing some students—creating the so-called pipeline from school to prison. They blame the schools, not their own policies that decimate social programs, allow children to experience the trauma of poverty, widen the chasm between the haves and have-nots, and underfund schools.

Ironically, the widespread experiment in distance learning caused by the COVID-19 pandemic may provide a partial solution. Distance or blended learning may be a way to provide an education to disruptive students unaffected by positive interventions. It may also improve instruction for the homebound and for those students who fail to thrive in the traditional school environment. Of course, this too will cost money that individual schools may not be able to allocate from their already inadequate budgets.

How do children who enter the public education system impact their schools and themselves? For some, the picture is bleak. Early childhood poverty negatively affects brain development, particularly in those areas that lead to academic success. This can be exacerbated by substance abuse and the influence of gangs. Modern technology is eroding social skills and the open-mindedness needed in a democratic society. There are few effective strategies for addressing the small percentage of students who disrupt schools.

All these negatives interrelate. Feelings of helplessness lead to gang affiliation. Poor social skills lead to bullying. Gangs use technology to communicate to escape detection and target victims.

These are the issues, basically societal and familial, that enter the schools. Teachers and principals have little control over these problems but are expected to solve them even when students are spending at least 80% of their waking hours interacting with peers, family, and their neighborhood environments.

Given additional funding, teaching, counseling, and social work staffs could be greatly expanded, particularly in early childhood, to provide one-on-one help to children and parents. Teachers at all levels could be given professional development on cognitive development and brain elasticity to help devise better instructional strategies. Such funding is not forthcoming.

The inclusion of social–emotional instruction could be greatly expanded, that is, if "the powers that be" would deemphasize testing so that schools could devote time to educating the whole child, instead of concentrating on test preparation. The testing mania shows no sign of diminishing.

Even if schools did get all the funding needed, it will have limited impact without governmental changes in policies regarding poverty, social inequality, blighted neighborhoods, homelessness and health care.

Let's look again at the statisticians that rate schools. They would probably discount all this as unmeasurable and stick to their tried-and-true analytics that emphasize testing over the education of the whole child.

Chapter Six

The Support Staff and a Foray into Bargaining Agreements

On any given day, every adult in a school will interact with dozens of students, parents, and visitors. Like teachers and school supervisory personnel, the support staff are in people-oriented jobs. In this age of ascribing a school's success or failure to teachers and school leaders, we must remember the key roles played by the support staff.

Supervisory and teaching staff are often in a state of flux (see Chapters 7 and 8), but the underlying bureaucracy of a school tends to be stable. This bureaucracy, composed of the nonpedagogical staff, impacts on a school's efficient running and the quality of services it provides to students, parents, and staff. Their work is often underestimated and therefore overlooked in school evaluations.

What constitutes "support staff" in a school? They are personnel not involved in the direct instruction of children or supervision of that instruction. Everyone in the school other than teachers, classroom paraprofessionals, assistant principals, department chairpersons, and principals are support staff.

First, we will look at secretaries, aides, safety agents or security guards, custodial staff, and lunchroom personnel. Then, we will examine the role of school guidance counselors, whose work supports student well-being and academic achievement. We will end this chapter with a foray into the issue of bargaining agreements, which determine some of the workplace rules for the operation and organization of a school.

When Ms. Wren took the reins of her elementary school, she found the school files in disarray. Student records were filed "holistically" under each letter of the alphabet. To find a specific transcript for a student with the last name Abreu, for example, all the "A" records were dumped on a desk and searched through. None of the records had been digitized, an on-

going district project. The longtime secretary told Ms. Wren it had always been done this way without any problems. She was also afraid of the newly installed computer. She had had no training in its use, nor did she understand the digitizing procedures.

As is the usual case with increased computerization, previously traditional jobs requiring pads, pencils, typewriters, and paper file folders now require technological expertise, everything from entering, accessing, and saving student records to preparing and submitting payrolls to ordering books and supplies and creating inventories. In larger schools, a secretary can specialize in one area; in smaller schools, they must be a Jack or Jill of all trades.

Experienced secretaries are aware of school procedures, required reports, protocols for helping sick students or staff, and procedures for conducting drills and setting up a command post in emergency situations. In the business world, the stereotype is true: the secretary often knows more about what is going on and how things are done than the CEO. The same is true in schools.

Secretaries are the face of the school—the first to answer the phone or greet a parent at an office desk and the first to talk to a student who has a problem or is ill or just needs to speak with a dean or counselor or school supervisor. How the secretary handles these initial face-to-face interactions may determine a parent's or child's perception of how much a school and its staff care.

Paid far less than teachers—and less than their corporate counterparts—secretaries, like teachers, set the tone for a school and need to have a unique set of people and management skills. Often, first-rate secretaries stay in the schools because the calendar allows them flexibility with their own childcare issues; or the hours and pressures are less than those in private businesses; or they enjoy working with children and helping supervisors and teachers in their important jobs; or, to put it simply, they like the school.

A small minority see a job with fewer workdays in the year and fewer hours each day with access to phones and computers so they can conduct other business. Principal Wren discovered that one secretary in her school was actually running a real estate business! Her predecessor had obviously been remiss in supervising the secretarial staff.

A newly assigned principal will inherit their secretary and the entire secretarial staff of the school. If the school is well run, much of the credit goes to these office managers, the glue of the school bureaucracy. If the school is not well run, the new principal needs to consider reassignment and professional development for the secretarial staff. This creates issues because the working conditions of secretaries in a school have been ossified by years of precedence.

Too often, a new principal, beset with dozens of other duties, allows past precedence to continue. This is a mistake. New principal Wren needs to:

- quickly assess the skills of the secretarial staff,
- create a job description for each secretarial slot in the school and align the positions to the skills of the secretaries she inherited,
- release appropriate secretaries to attend staff development on new procedures being instituted by the district,
- create monitoring procedures to ensure secretarial time is being used appropriately, and
- ensure that the school is a pleasant workplace to retain good secretaries.

A principal may find that a secretary neither wants to change past precedent nor has the personality or the skills needed for the positions available. The principal will have to consult the secretaries' bargaining agreement regarding provisions for transfer or removal. All this takes a great deal of time, effort, and negotiation. It could take several years before the needed modifications are in place.

Principals must acknowledge the importance of the secretarial staff and ensure everyone in the school is aware of their contributions.

A few years into her principalship, Ms. Wren was conducting the first in a series of new teacher workshops. She asked the participants who was the most important person in the school. Answers included the custodian; their immediate supervisor; and, of course, the principal. She disagreed, noting that for them the most important person was her secretary, whom she referred to as her "office manager." She gave two reasons.

First, she trusted her secretary with initial review of job applications. If any had grammatical errors, misinformation (as misspelling the school's name), or smudges or stains, the secretary put them in the "secondary pile."

Second, the secretary assessed each of them on their courtesy, demeanor, and dress when they came for an interview and gave Ms. Wren her candid evaluation before the interview began. In short, none present would have their current jobs if they hadn't passed the secretary's muster. In addition, the secretary was the unofficial gatekeeper of the office, and her opinion of a teacher would determine a teacher's access to the principal.

The second most important person was the payroll secretary, who gave good advice on how to apply for salary differentials and completed the biweekly payroll that would get them paid. Ms. Wren went on to explain that sometimes teachers considered secretaries second-class citizens, there to serve teacher needs and provide immediate gratification. Teachers with such an attitude should realize that nothing in a school gets done without the secretarial staff—and where their needs fell on the long priority list would be determined by their attitudes.

Ms. Wren, remembering her own advice, hosted a "Secretary Appreciation Day" every June.

The range of duties assigned to school aides is enormous: guarding entry/exit points, taking door attendance, monitoring the lunchroom, duplicating materials, storing and delivering supplies, answering telephones, and helping in the library. Often, the lowest-paid employees in the school, they save substantial budgetary dollars by enabling the more highly paid professional staff to concentrate on instruction, rather than handling day-to-day minutiae.

School aides (like lunchroom workers) are usually from the immediate community, making them valuable sources of local information and often providing familiar faces for the children. Most are high school graduates without any pedagogical training. Their interpersonal skills will vary. Just as with secretaries, it is important to create job descriptions to define the responsibilities of each.

This is relatively easy because there are few restrictions on what a school aide can do as long as long as it is a task needed by the school and does not infringe on duties specified in the secretaries' contract. In some districts, new principals may find that they must keep the aide staff inherited due to contractual seniority rules. Those with poor interpersonal skills need to be placed in jobs that minimize contact with students (as duplicating materials or handling supplies and inventory) and others assigned according to their talents and demeanor.

Principal Joaquin found that Jason had been hired as a school aide over sixteen years ago. It did not take long for him to realize that he had special needs and sometimes got confused and angry when faced with conflicting requests. He handled supply delivery—books, paper, erasers, pencils, and binders—to classrooms and offices. Teachers would see him in the hall and ask for this or that, and he would drop whatever he was doing to accommodate them and then forget what he was originally doing.

A new assistant principal of operations wanted Jason removed. He did not record all his extra deliveries, so the inventory was not updated. He did not make deliveries and sometimes left materials on a cart in a hallway. When two teachers would come at him with requests at the same time, he sometimes "lost it" and ran off.

Mr. Joaquin worked with the AP to solve these problems. Simple request forms for supplies were created. All requests went to the assistant principal, who signed off on the form, which was then given to Jason. When he made a delivery, the staff member signed the form, which Jason then gave back to the AP. All staff were made aware of the procedures. Jason carried extra request forms to give to anyone wanting supplies. He practiced what to say: "Please complete this form and give it to Ms._____for approval."

When possible, it is best to work with the aide staff you have, people who have been with the school for a long time and have loyalty to its efficient operation. Because of the flexibility within assignments, it is not difficult to match the person to the job.

It is equally important that the professional staff not treat school aides as lackeys at their beck and call for whatever they need. Teachers need to be made aware of the procedures the various school aides must follow and understand that without their help nothing would be duplicated for their use, no supplies would be delivered, and there would be lax supervision at school entry points and less assistance in offices.

In the past, schools were considered safe havens for students and staff. There was little fear of violence outside the hormonal tantrums of maturing children. Today, weapons, especially guns, have become commonplace, and schools are targets. The role of security guards has changed. The once friendly greeters of students and visitors have been replaced by trained security teams, often armed and part of the local police force and not under the direct supervision of the principal. Some students begin their day walking through metal detectors.

What does the increased presence of school security mean? Let's look at the data.

Over 90% of schools have controlled access to buildings during school hours. Over 80% use security cameras. Over 65% require faculty and staff to wear badges or picture IDs. Relatively few schools require students to wear badges or picture IDs: 2.9% of primary schools, 13.0% of middle schools, and 16.2% of high schools. Relatively few have random metal detector checks: 2.0% of primary schools, 7.1% of middle schools, and 10.6% of high schools (National Center for Education Statistics 2019c).

School security staffs have increased, as has the percentage carrying firearms. See Table 6.1.

When improved behavioral strategies are implemented, this increase in school security parallels decreases in school crime. "Between 2001 and 2017, the percentage of students ages 12–18 who reported being victimized at school during the previous 6 months decreased overall (from 6 to 2 percent), as did the percentages of students who reported theft (from 4 to 1 percent) and violent victimization (from 2 to 1 percent)" (National Center for Education Statistics n.d.a).

Table 6.1. Data on School Security Staffs

School Characteristic	Percentage with One or More Security Staff		Percentage with a Security Staff Routinely Carrying a firearm*	
	2005–2006	2015–2016	2005–2006	2015–2016
All Public Schools	41.7	56.5	30.7	42.9
Primary Schools	26.2	45.4	15.7	30.6
Middle Schools	63.7	73.4	51.8	60.0
High Schools	75.2	81.0	64.0	70.9
Locale				
City	49.1	61.9	30.5	36.0
Suburban	42.7	57.9	32.2	44.6
Town	44.4	62.0	38.1	56.5
Rural	33.8	46.7	27.1	41.3

*"Prior to 2015-16, the School Survey on Crime and Safety (SSOCS) questionnaire asked respondents whether any of the security guards, security personnel, or sworn law enforcement officers at their school routinely carried a firearm. The 2015-16 SSOCS questionnaire asked respondents only whether any of the sworn law enforcement officers (including SROs) at their school routinely carried a firearm; therefore, direct comparisons with earlier years should be avoided. Data on security staff routinely carrying a firearm were not collected in the 2013-14 Fast Response Survey System (FRSS)" (National Center for Education Statistics n.d.d).

According to the same study, bullying also declined. The percentage of students who reported being bullied at school during the school year decreased from 29% in 2005 to 20% in 2017.

School guards are a major factor in making schools safe places for students and staff. They handle door security; patrol school hallways, lunchrooms, and athletic areas; collaborate with the deans and other school security personnel; and are often the first called when a potentially dangerous situation arises.

School guard Belinda was stationed at the main entrance of the school. It was her job to be sure all visitors identified themselves, signed in, were given name tags, and waited until school personnel escorted them to the appropriate office. Unfortunately, Belinda lacked people skills.

Her first words to visitors were usually "Who are you?" When visitors did not have photo IDs, she berated them and barred them from entry, even when the school had requested their presence to meet with a staff member. On more than one occasion, verbal arguments came close to escalating into physical altercations.

The principal conferred with the district security chief and other district principals having similar issues with some of their guards. Together, they wrote a script for the guards to use. The also created workshops to be delivered at the district office. Principals would follow up in their schools. The security of students and staff remained a priority, but parents and other legiti-

mate visitors would now be greeted politely and, using the protocols created, be able to gain entry to meet with the appropriate staff member.

Principals rarely hire the security staff. This is usually done by the district and in some major cities by the police department. Every school is different and has a different culture and ambience. Security guards are given generic training and then randomly assigned to schools. Few are trained in child and adolescent psychology or on how to interact with children of varying ages. Periodically, they are rotated to different schools. Some children fear security guards, whose uniforms mirror those of police officers. Some see them as officials who want to have them or their parents deported.

Working with the security staff is a delicate task for principals, who must maintain the culture and ambience of their schools while working with guards they did not hire and often do not supervise. This requires time, effort, and tact, adding yet another layer of responsibility to the duties of the principal. Principals can:

- deal with the gaps in training, integrating security guards into the school security team with deans and guidance counselors and seeking their input and expertise regarding school safety plans and emergency procedures;
- work directly with their local police departments and local commanders (and/or with district supervisors) by meeting with them regularly to discuss the role of school guards and the needs of their particular schools;
- try to establish protocols that satisfy the parameters of school safety while meeting the needs of students, parents, and staff;
- invite members of the local police to school events, such as performances, dances, and parent nights; and
- ask members of the local police to visit school classrooms to talk to students about their profession and how they and the students can work together to make the school and community safer places.

The cafeteria is at the heart of most schools. Almost every student goes there every day. It is a place to unwind and relax. The school administration can do many things to make this period of the day safe and more pleasant. It can ensure safety and security, provide recreation in the form of board games, and create a more welcoming atmosphere by brightening up the usually drab walls with murals created by talented students.

The center of the cafeteria is the kitchen and food service area, usually supervised by the school dietician. The generic term "cafeteria workers" describes those who assist with food preparation and those who serve the students. None of them are hired or supervised by the principal, but, on any given day, any one of them could affect the life of a child.

Maria, who lived in the community, was a cafeteria worker in a middle school for over twenty years. She started when her own children were in school as a way to supplement the family income but found that she liked interacting with students, especially those she recognized from the neighborhood. When time permitted, she engaged the children in conversation.

She noticed that Miguel was taking less and less food each day. His previously pleasant conversations with her at the service area were now low mumbles. Maria thought he looked sickly. Toward the end of the lunch period, she spoke with the cafeteria dean, who in turn spoke to Miguel's guidance counselor. Because of Maria's intervention, Miguel began treatment for anorexia. When the principal, Mr. Joaquin, was made aware of this, he met with the school dietician to set up a workshop on recognizing the symptoms of eating disorders for all cafeteria workers. He also sent a letter of commendation to Maria.

Principals have always worked with school dieticians regarding the scheduling of lunch periods, providing lunch for students going on trips and catering special school events. Together, they enforce district regulations banning non-nutritious snacks. The lunchroom also is an important place in the school where a caring adult's interaction with a child can make that child's day or, as in the anecdote above, save a child's life.

We generally talk about how teachers, counselors, and school leaders impact on the lives of students. Savvy principals know that any of the scores of other adults in the building, from cafeteria workers to school aides to security guards, also interact with children and that any one of them could become the go-to person for a child. They must be provided with training in interacting with children, district regulations, and school protocols.

A student comes to the school filled with rage. The suicide rate among young people continues to rise, and the age of the children keeps falling. The New York State legislature considered a bill to allow students to take "mental health days" to combat student depression. Eating disorders, substance abuse, and the opioid epidemic are serious problems.

While teachers may be among the professionals on the front line to recognize the signs and symptoms, it will be the school guidance counselors who work one-on-one with the children and their parents and, when necessary, make appropriate referrals to out-of-school agencies.

The American School Counselor Association (https://www.schoolcounselor.org/) recommends a counselor-to-student ratio of 250:1. As of the 2017–2018 school year, only two states, New Hampshire and Vermont, met this recommendation. Nationwide, the ratio is 442:1. In some states, it is much higher: Arizona, 925:1; Michigan, 725:1; Minnesota, 669:1; and California 644:1 (American School Counselor Association n.d.).

When Ms. Rayne became principal of her high school of about 1,600 students, there were two full-time guidance counselors. The retiring principal told her that counselors were a waste of money. They sat in their offices reading newspapers, never responded to teacher referrals, and did not improve test scores.

Her own observation showed that, with a caseload of 800 students, each counselor was overwhelmed and could do only crisis counseling, dealing with one serious issue after another. There was no procedure for sending follow-ups to the teachers who made referrals, leading the teachers to think that the counselors did nothing but return troubled children to their classrooms.

She found that some guidance responsibilities (academic performance checks and student and parental notifications of the same) were done by teachers given a reduced teaching load. She eliminated this practice and slightly increased average class size (within contractual limits). With the savings, Ms. Rayne was able to hire two more guidance counselors, cutting caseloads in half.

She met with the counselors and laid out new ground rules.

First, staff members who referred students had to receive notification the children had been seen and given as much information as allowed about how they should follow up in the classroom.

Second, counselors would be reorganized to stay with a class, following the same students from ninth through twelfth grades. They would meet with each student each semester to review academic performance and make it clear where each stood; they would probe for any underlying issues that could be addressed before they reached the crisis stage.

Third, they would engage in whole-class and small-group sessions as well as individual counseling so that appropriate information could be delivered efficiently.

Fourth, they would facilitate workshops for staff at professional development meetings to alert them to warning signs of problems and make them aware of the role of the counselor.

The new configuration worked. Two years later, a fifth counselor was hired to handle college and career counseling.

Guidance counselors are experts at working with children individually and in small groups. They counsel children facing problems that impact on school performance, from dealing with the death of loved ones to bullying, eating disorders, thoughts of suicide, family dysfunction, and every type of fear and anxiety.

Counselors are the advocates for children in the school and should be partners with teachers, yet the two are sometimes at odds with each other. Sometimes, teachers think that counselors "coddle" children and send them back to class without proper admonitions. Sometimes, counselors feel teachers do not spend enough time with the child to understand their specific needs and problems.

In the not so distant past, most school counselors were former teachers who chose counseling as their next career pathway. Having been in the classroom, they understood the pressures faced by teachers dealing with twenty or thirty-plus children per class for most of the school day. Most of today's counselors have never taught, so they lack the perspective of the classroom teacher—a perspective they need.

Likewise, classroom teachers have little idea what counselors do. They know they refer children and that children return to their classes and sometimes engage in the same poor behaviors. They know that while they are working with groups of children in a large classroom, counselors work one-on-one in private or semiprivate offices; sometimes, they are alone in these offices, seemingly not working that hard. There is professional jealously because teachers are human.

What can be done?

First, the same professional development given to first-year teachers should include first-year counselors. During discussions, each will gain an understanding of the other's perspective and better understand one another's responsibilities. One session for new hires should include a presentation on the guidance program of the school.

Second, have guidance counselors experience what it is like to teach a class. Counselors could visit fifth-grade classes to talk about the transition to middle school or visit ninth-grade classes to discuss what a GPA is and how it will affect college admissions. Information will be conveyed efficiently, and the counselor will learn what it is like to work with thirty or so students at the same time. Of course, they should receive PD prior to addressing a class.

Third, as previously noted, counselors could run professional development sessions for teachers to help them learn the signs of students in trouble and explain the referral process. Then, they could discuss how they address these issues with the students—giving teachers a counselor's perspective.

Finally, schools need funding to support a full guidance staff. Many problems go unaddressed because counselors have impossible caseloads and cannot meet with students in a timely fashion. While a ratio of 250:1 is the ideal, fewer would be better. In our world of underfunding, few schools can afford this. Many elementary schools may not even have a full-time counselor. When a premium is put on passing examinations, the main goal is maximizing classroom instruction in tested subject areas, so a teacher in the classroom is seen as having more "value" than a counselor in an office.

The paucity of funding forces principals to make difficult staffing decisions. Counselors are often stymied by the scarcity of social service agencies to which they can refer parents and students because governments at all levels provide inadequate funding for these critical agencies. The problem is exacerbated in high-poverty areas.

In addition to working with children, counselors are an important part of the school bureaucracy, completing required reports on everything from suicide attempts to pregnancies to students living in shelters. They are often the point persons for reports of child abuse or neglect. They complete credit checks and inform students and parents regarding deficiencies. They send letters to the parents of children in danger of not advancing or not graduating and set up meetings to discuss problems. They keep records of the same for summary reports.

The record-keeping and reporting aspect of the position are professional responsibilities, but they often have low priority compared to the day-to-day needs of students. Sometimes, additional funding and support depends on the reports. A reasonable caseload would help as would professional development in time management, record keeping, and report completion.

Principals are the rating officers for guidance counselors and have the ability to ensure that they function competently. Most principals come from the ranks of teachers and have little awareness of the roles of counselors. They are overwhelmed by the time and effort they must devote to observing, training, and rating classroom teachers and completing a myriad of investigative reports. So what always was tends to continue to be regarding counselors. As a result, few, if any, of the recommendations made above are implemented.

There are other professional support staff in some schools who deserve mention for the important work they do.

Many student issues are home issues, so a school social worker can play an important role in the overall well-being of the students and their families. Schools that serve students with special needs have full- or part-time psychologists as well as occupational, speech, and physical therapists. They are usually assigned by the district to serve specific students and are funded separately; that is, their cost does not come out of the school's budget. Additional social workers and school psychologists would complement the work of counselors, but few schools can afford them.

As mentioned in Chapter 3, schools with a medical office may have a full- or part-time school nurse. Some are funded by the district so that required vision and hearing screenings can be done. In some large cities, they are funded by municipal hospitals, which find that having a nurse and even a doctor in a school relieves the pressure on emergency rooms and allows for early diagnosis and treatment of chronic diseases. Having on-site medical staff reduces instructional time lost by ill or injured students.

On-site medical personnel are a positive trend that helps students and schools while costing the school nothing except some space. Despite this, there is a lack of funding for such on-site help.

As we segue from the support staff to the teaching and supervisory staff in the next two chapters, let's take a brief look at bargaining agreements. Contracts have been blamed for everything that is bad in schools, especially for protecting ineffective school personnel. As usual, the public, politicians, and the media have it wrong.

First, we are not looking at any one contract but several involving different bargaining units. Custodians may be represented by one union, cafeteria workers by another, and aides by yet another. Teachers are represented by one bargaining unit and supervisory staff by another. Secretaries, guidance counselors, and social workers may be part of the teachers' bargaining unit or not.

Second, the larger the school district, the lengthier and more complex the contracts. Let's look at the lengths of some recent teacher contracts: Chicago, 456 pages; Los Angeles, 406; New York City, 238; Jefferson County, Kentucky, 101; Brevard County, Florida, 92; and Des Moines, 43. For information on scores of school districts and links to teacher contracts, go to Teacher Contract Database, National Council on Teacher Quality, https://www.nctq.org/contract-database.

Third, contracts and unions are not negatives. Unions seek higher salaries for underpaid school personnel, from school aides to principals. Union contracts try to improve working conditions, which in turn, helps with staff recruitment and retention. They also provide for due process so that employees cannot be summarily dismissed. Some pundits feel due process is cumbersome and keeps ineffective personnel in a school. This is not the case. Due process defines the rules for all parties and specifies the necessary documentation needed for dismissal. Sometimes, the supervisor in charge fails to follow procedures or have the proper documentation. The fault lies with the supervisor, not the process.

Contracts are not the problem. The way many are negotiated may be. Let's look at contract negotiations in large school districts, usually in urban areas. Those representing the district are often professional negotiators who are trying to keep costs down while raising productivity. In many cases, they are not educators and know very little about how schools operate. Let's look at what might result from this.

A district's bargaining unit was willing to relieve teachers of nonprofessional duties in exchange for more time for curriculum writing and review, collaboration, and increased parental contact. The teachers' union was in full agreement, and the dreaded and decidedly unprofessional chore of lunchroom duty was eliminated from the contract. What did this mean for principals?

- Principals in large schools that had three or four lunch periods had to make sure there was an adult presence, at least two school aides, meaning

the cost of six to eight hours of school aide salary per day, 1,200 to 1,600 hours per year.
- As lunchrooms can be a source of problems with 300 to 500 students together at one time, most principals would also want a "cafeteria dean" to supervise the school aides and bring a teacher's interpersonal skills into the mix. The cost: three or four time-compensated periods per day, 600 to 800 per year.
- The curriculum writing and review would require training so that all the teachers involved would be on the same page. The new professional duties would need to be monitored with sign-in sheets, summaries, and lists of parents called. If the contract negotiated called for it, reports on all this would have to be made to the designated authority. These become new responsibilities of the supervisory staff.

Was this a good contract provision for teachers and students? Yes. But it also added to the budgetary problems and supervisory responsibilities of the principal and assistant principals. Would the district provide more funding or additional supervisory support? Of course not.

Another issue that might be negotiated would be parameters for beginning and ending the school day. Teachers in urban and suburban schools always want to begin and end early to reduce rush hour car or public transportation delays. Yet research tells us that children are on a different clock than adults and do better with later starts and endings. A principal wanting to implement what the research says would be stymied if district negotiators had agreed to an early start to the school day or left this up to a vote of the teachers in the school.

Contracts also may impose restrictions on programming with limitations on how teachers are assigned classes: number of assignments in a row, number of preps, and use of seniority for program preferences. These are important aspects of teacher contracts, but there should be room for flexibility and in-school variations, especially with the growing number of small schools where program parameters are limited by the number of students enrolled.

A principal has to deal with more than just the teacher's contract. The secretaries in a district were able to negotiate that they would not be required to watch children in elementary schools, as this was not a secretary's responsibility. They were right. However, it was common practice at the end of the school day for children not picked up by their parents to be brought to the principal's office until the parent or designated guardian arrived, sometimes thirty or sixty minutes later.

Because of this seemingly innocuous contract provision, the principal had to find money to fund an "after-school homework class" where a teacher was paid per session to supervise and assist the children until the parents arrived. This was probably a better system than leaving students in the principal's office, but a costly one—about 200 per-session hours per year.

Other contracts also impact on the operation of the school. What are the school opening and closing times specified in the custodian's contract? Will the school be charged additional fees for late afternoon or evening activities, such as basketball team practices and games, parent meetings, back-to-school nights, or dramatic or orchestral performances? Does the contract call for the sorting of trash to conform to the community's recycling ordinances? How often is ordinary maintenance, such as painting school interiors, done?

What are the contract-specified working hours for school security personnel? No one can enter the school, such as teachers arriving early to prepare lessons or students for tutoring, until security personnel are present and entry procedures in place. Likewise, at what point does the guards' day end and security overtime paid out of the school budget?

All contracts impact on the operation and budget of the school. Each bargaining unit—teachers, secretaries, custodians, and security personnel—has a say in what it seeks for its members. Principals have a say only in their own contracts, but their ability to manage a school and its budget is impacted—for better or worse—by the contracts negotiated by all other bargaining units in the school. It might make sense for those negotiating for the district to seek the input of principals before agreeing to new contractual provisions. Will this happen? Probably not.

Principals can exert considerable influence over the nonteaching staff, with time, tact, and possible reorganizations and reassignments. Such time is a valuable commodity when the mandated priority is instruction, assessment, and improving test scores.

Principals have no control over the contracts of the people who work in the school. They must abide by provisions too often negotiated by noneducators. This can make scheduling and programming more complex and be a strain on an already overstretched budget. As we learned in Chapter 2, principals are given a budget, often with many restrictions, and must organize a school within its parameters. This leads to difficult personnel decisions regarding the needs for teaching staff, counselors, social workers, and school aides.

Do the analytics used to evaluate the school take the lack of funding to increase the counselor-to-student ratio into consideration? Do they incorporate a statistic to measure the impact of the various contracts on the operation of the school? Do they take into consideration the amount of time a principal must devote to reorganizing, training, and monitoring the nonpedagogical staff? Such questions are rhetorical.

Chapter Seven

Teachers

Teachers are on the front lines of the struggle to raise student achievement and improve schools. Without their dedication and hard work, nothing can change.

The profession of teaching is in crisis. Enrollment in schools of education is shrinking. The education provided by those schools and alternative certification programs is being questioned. A large percentage of teachers leave the profession each year. Salaries are not commensurate with a teacher's responsibility and paltry compared with other professions. Teachers feel their ability to teach is being shackled by "the powers that be." The prestige of the profession is tumbling.

At the same time, teachers are being bombarded by mounds of data and held ever more accountable for the achievement of their students as the factors of parenting; disruptive children; deteriorating physical plants; and interference by districts, states, and politicians are discounted. They are being charged with educating students to change society while the poverty and income inequality of that very society are deepening and negatively impacting on the work they do.

Let's explore this crisis in teaching and see what, if anything, can be done.

The literary and cinematic portrayal of teachers gives the public an unrealistic view of the profession. Mr. Chips is the epitome of such a portrayal—the young idealistic teacher who stays with the profession through thick and thin, ending his career as the venerable old school master with fond memories of all the students he helped through the decades.

Mr. Holland's Opus updates the story. Here, a venerable music teacher is forced into retirement by budget cuts. But wait! His former instrumental music students come together for a final performance of the masterpiece he never published. Other inspirational movies include *Blackboard Jungle, To*

Sir with Love, and *Stand and Deliver*. On television, we went from the idealism of Mr. Novak and *Room 222* to the wise-cracking but good-hearted Mr. Kotter to the teacher as superhero in the *Greatest American Hero*.

In more recent years, educators have taken on more negative personae in movies, such as *Fast Times at Ridgemont High*, *Teachers*, and *Bad Teacher*, and on TV shows, such as *Boston Public*, where just about every action of the principal would have led to his dismissal in most school districts.

Neither extreme is an accurate depiction of real people trying to do one of the last person-to-person jobs. The crisis in teaching is so critical that it was the cover story on an installment of the national news magazine *CBS Sunday Morning* (Hudespeth 2019). This news segment begins with a statistic:

> Nationwide about one in five teachers (or 18%) has a second job during the academic year, which is not so surprising when you consider that, since 1996, inflation-adjusted pay for a public school teacher has actually *fallen* by 1.7%. The average annual teacher salary today: just over $60,000, with nearly a third of teachers (31%) making less than $45,000 a year.

Money issues are further explored through interviews with two teachers in Oklahoma, a state with one of the lowest teacher pay rates. A veteran of fifteen years—who worked another job while teaching—left the profession to take a factory job. He earns $12,000 a year more than he made teaching.

A tearful high school English teacher related how her department lost twenty-six teachers in the past five and a half years. She added, "And the most painful part is that students are the ones who feel it. Like, they get attached to those teachers. They look forward to having them."

Dana Goldstein, author of *The Teacher Wars: A History of America's Most Embattled Profession* (2014), was interviewed. She related low teacher salaries to the early history of public education: "When it came time to have universal public education for all American kids, Horace Mann, the father of our public school system, said, 'I have an idea: Let's bring women in as teachers. Then we can expand public education and it will not cost quite as much.'" Why? In the early 1800s it was legal to pay women half as much as men. Similar ideas persisted into the 20th century.

According to the CBS news segment, time and respect are two other major issues plaguing teachers. The veteran who took the factory job noted: "When I first started teaching, like, you might have one meeting a month. When I left, you would have two meetings a week. You'd also have two meetings during the school day. You might have one before. And the amount of paperwork is insane."

Dana Goldstein noted that many teachers just don't feel respected. She traced this back to the 1983 report *A Nation at Risk*, which, she says, argued that "teachers, and the sort of low-intellectual capacity of some teachers, was to blame for kids having low test scores and not being able to compete internationally." She added: "It was a big change. And I think for many teachers that was the beginning of feeling that they were being unfairly portrayed and unfairly treated by policy makers, by politicians."

This led to the beginning of increased paperwork teachers complain about: "As new mandates to improve test scores, track student progress, and justify every lesson were piling up, everyone else, it seemed, piled it on."

In today's world where news from legitimate sources is called "fake news" and there is always a suspicion that producers and reporters have political biases, it is important that we fact check this TV news story.

The crisis in teaching is documented in "Teacher Shortages Worsening in the Majority of US States, Study Reveals" (Betancourt 2018). *The Guardian* contacted the departments and boards of education of every state. Nine either did not respond or did not provide the information or data requested. Of the forty-one states responding, twenty-eight said they were experiencing a teacher shortage, and fifteen said this shortage had gotten worse in the past year. "Schools are struggling to fill positions in science, special education and mathematics and often have trouble keeping teachers because of low salaries, high student loans and reduced budgets."

As a result, "less effective teachers are in the classroom" as states resort to short-term licensure, which allows uncertified teachers to complete requirements while on the job. This takes many forms. In California, there are PIPs (teachers on provisional intern permits) and STSPs (short-term staff permits). The state has 4,000 teachers in one of these categories. "Oklahoma is beginning with nearly 500 teaching vacancies—despite the heavy reliance on underqualified emergency instructors." South Dakota and Rhode Island have similar problems (Betancourt 2018).

"But even with intensive recruiting both in and outside of the country, more than 100,000 classrooms are being staffed this year by instructors who are unqualified for their jobs" (Strauss 2017a). She adds, "Not only are underprepared teachers less effective on average, they are also 2 to 3 times more likely to leave teaching than fully prepared teachers, creating a revolving door that makes solving shortages an uphill climb."

Another reason for the teacher shortage is that we no longer live in the age of Horace Mann and the many talented women who previously filled the ranks of the profession, especially in the elementary grades, have found more lucrative jobs elsewhere.

When Mr. Joaquin became an assistant principal in 1986, he found that his veteran female teachers were top notch—extremely smart, organized, and dedicated. During a conversation with Mrs. O'Connell, the reading specialist, he asked why she entered the profession. Her response: For her generation of middle-class children coming of age in the early 1950s, there were few viable options for talented women: housewife, secretary, nurse, or teacher. Had she been born even ten years later, she would have aspired to become a lawyer or doctor or stockbroker. As he thought about this, Mr. Joaquin realized that the most efficient school secretaries he had encountered were also of Ms. O'Connell's generation.

Mr. Joaquin wonders whether perhaps part of the growing crises in education is that newer generations of the most capable women, having more lucrative career choices, are no longer entering into the relatively low-paying and low-prestige teaching or school secretary professions.

To make ends meet, one in six teachers work second jobs (Schaffer 2019). Citing Bureau of Labor Statistics, she notes that "teachers [are] about three times as likely as U.S. workers overall to balance multiple jobs."

Schaffer goes on to say, "On average, a teacher's summer job earnings account for 7% of their total annual income, according to the NCES [National Center for Educational Statistics] data. Earnings from a second job during the school year make up an average of 9% of their income." The less experienced the teacher, the more likely they have a summer or after-school job. In other words, those teachers who are still learning their craft are more likely to have less time to devote to lesson preparation because they need a second job.

The *Washington Post* reports: "While teacher shortages are not new, they are getting worse in many parts of the country. A report by the nonprofit Learning Policy Institute found that teacher education enrollment dropped from 691,000 to 451,000, a 35 percent reduction, between 2009 and 2014—and nearly 8 percent of the teaching workforce is leaving every year, the majority before retirement age" (Strauss 2017a).

The article "Broad Discontent Leads Half of Teachers to Consider Quitting Their Jobs" (2019) gives us the following data, based on a poll of a national random sample of public school teachers:

- Only 39% feel their pay is fair, and this percentage is skewed because, while 60% of teachers in the Northeast and 47% in the West feel their pay is fair, teachers in other parts of the nation have far lower percentages.
- Forty-eight percent feel less valued by the community.
- Fifty percent have seriously considered leaving the profession.

Other factors are also cited. A significant percentage of teachers say they consider leaving the profession because of stress/burnout/pressure (19%), lack of respect/feeling valued (10%), student behavior (9%), and school administrators/board (7%) ("Broad Discontent Leads Half of Teachers to Consider Quitting Their Jobs" 2019, K7).

Santoro probes deeper into the concept of teacher burnout. She writes about "demoralization" when teachers become "frustrated because they could not teach the way they believed was right." She adds: "Demoralization is a professional not a personal problem due to the context and conditions of work, rather than deficiencies in the individual teacher" (Santoro 2020, 30).

Santoro recounts anecdotal stories involving several teachers, citing reasons for their demoralization and, sometimes, moral dilemmas. One felt her instruction was being dumbed down to meet curriculum mandates and that the district prioritized "procedural compliance over deep learning." Another, dealing with a "rotating cast of principals," felt pressured to pass students, in other words, "to be mindful of publicly available statistics and their consequences."

A third teacher felt that school leaders and hired consultants "left teachers voiceless and morally suspect if they asked critical questions" (Santoro 2020, 30–32).

A Graide Network blog summarizes all these factors ("Why Some States Have Higher Teacher Turnover Rates than Others" 2019):

> Why do so many teachers end up leaving the field of education? A number of studies and surveys have been done over the years to answer this question. Some of the most common answers are:
>
> - Emotional exhaustion/stress/burnout
> - Challenging work conditions and long hours
> - Low pay
> - Not enough support or respect
> - Overemphasis on high-stakes testing
> - Schools are no longer looking out for kids' best interests
> - In the end, family takes priority

It would seem that the *CBS Sunday Morning* news magazine was on target with its report.

The COVID-19 pandemic could make the crisis in teaching much worse. As we saw in Chapter 2, without massive funds from the federal government, hundreds of thousands of teaching jobs are being lost because of the cost of the pandemic to the states. Even if this funding materializes, the teacher shortage could deepen.

Education Week Teacher reports: "Two-thirds of educators say they're concerned about the health implications of resuming in-person instruction in the fall, and some say the coronavirus outbreak—and its dramatic effects on schooling—has increased the likelihood that they will leave the classroom altogether (Will 2020). Citing federal data, Will notes that 18% of teachers are older than fifty-five, putting them in the at-risk category; 36% have a health condition that puts them at risk; and "nearly 70 percent said a loved one, who they either live with or see regularly, has a high-risk condition."

What might this mean? Citing a recent EdWeek Research Center survey, Will notes that 20% of the teachers surveyed said they are now "somewhat more" or "much more" likely to leave classroom teaching at the end of the (2019–2020) school year, compared to 9% who said this before the coronavirus outbreak.

The article goes on to say that the pandemic might also be adding to teacher dissatisfaction. Susan Moore Johnson, a Harvard University professor of education who studies teachers' work conditions and satisfaction, is cited. She thinks negative feelings by teachers may be exacerbated by the COVID crisis. "I think it's very unclear, at this point, whether teachers will feel as if they are being treated as professionals, and if they are going to be able to do the kinds of teaching that they prefer, which is essentially interactive and social rather than following more prescriptions and doing it at a distance," Johnson said (Will 2020).

What impact will COVID-19 have on classrooms in the 2020–2021 school year and thereafter? Will the age and medical conditions of teachers and/or their loved ones double the already high rate of attrition leading to many more uncertified and underprepared teachers in our classrooms? Or will possible budget cuts mean they will not be replaced and even more will be laid off, having a catastrophic effect on the education of children?

We live in an atmosphere of distrust—of government, of legal systems, of police departments, of once admired organizations, of corporations. From the highest echelons of the government, we hear facts ignored and obvious lies denied. The public sees that once esteemed organizations, from the Boy Scouts to churches and synagogues, ignored the abuse of children for decades. Corporations, such as Enron, Wells Fargo, and Perdue Pharmaceuticals, were all in one way or another fleecing the public.

It's not that such corruption is new—it has always existed. But, for the past twenty years, the growth of instant communication and internet support groups has made the public more aware of illegalities and foibles. The rise of fringe groups and conspiracy theorists has made this much worse, finding issues that do not exist, further eroding public trust.

As was pointed out, *A Nation at Risk* shed public doubt on teachers. This goes much deeper. As children are raised with the idea that they are all winners and can do no wrong, responsibility for their misbehavior or failure is ascribed to their teachers. As the sense of personal responsibility declines, finger-pointing at others increases.

All K–12 educators are under the scrutiny of politicians, press, and parents looking for political capital, soundbites, and someone to blame for poor student behavior and achievement. Teachers (and school leaders) constantly second-guess themselves about everything they say or do. Will telling a student that their paper was plagiarized lead to an allegation of verbal abuse? Will restraining a student running wildly down the staircase become an allegation of corporal punishment?

Over twenty years ago, high school principal Ms. Rayne saw the handwriting on the wall as regulations regarding staff misbehavior were rewritten and investigations of corporal punishment and verbal abuse rose dramatically. Every year, at the opening September conference, she said to her teachers, "In today's educational climate, it is healthy to be a little bit paranoid." She went on to explain the regulations that required that every allegation be investigated and then noted in the teacher's file, even if it were found to have no basis. She concluded, "Remember, today's congratulatory pat on the back could be tomorrow's repressed memory of inappropriate touching."

What would Ms. Rayne say to her staff in today's world of Facebook, YouTube, Instagram, and Twitter?

Before we move on to ideas for the better recruitment and retention of teachers, let's look at teacher preparation.

Teacher preparation programs in the US are hit and miss. Each state has its own certification process, and each institution of higher learning creates its own program within state-mandated parameters. There are a variety of alternative certification programs. States create special programs to be sure there are teachers in shortage areas. There are few quality controls.

In 2014, the US Department of Education recognized this, quoting then US Education Secretary Arne Duncan: "It has long been clear that as a nation, we could do a far better job of preparing teachers for the classroom. It's not just something that studies show—I hear it in my conversations with teachers, principals and parents. New teachers want to do a great job for their kids, but often, they struggle at the beginning of their careers and have to figure out too much for themselves. Teachers deserve better, and our students do too" ("US Department of Education Proposes Plan to Strengthen Teacher Preparation" 2014).

Guidelines were determined. Little changed. The National Council on Teacher Quality (NCTQ) reviews graduate and alternative teacher preparation programs in the US, applying a variety of standards. The 2018 summary states: "The ratings highlight the disconnect between the preparation teachers receive and the real demands of teaching." These ratings document vast differences in the quality of teacher preparation programs, traditional and alternative, in individual institutions and states as a whole.

The NCTQ report makes the following points:

- "While nothing in the structure of graduate or alternative route programs inherently hinders them from being selective, too many simply are not. Too many imply that teaching is easy, that anyone can do it, by admitting almost everyone with minimal application requirements. Just 14 percent of traditional and 23 percent of alternative certification programs have rigorous admissions criteria" (Rickenbrode et al. 2018, 4).
- "On the graduate side, just 15 percent have adequate minimal expectations regarding the academic backgrounds in history, literature, and science that applicants should bring to the program and, even worse, just one percent require adequate knowledge in mathematics" (Rickenbrode et al. 2018, 3).
- "Too many programs provide inadequate practice before licensure—neglecting to take advantage of opportunities to place student teachers and residents in the classrooms of expert, effective mentor teachers, and failing to frequently observe the novices" (Rickenbrode et al. 2018, 2).

Let's look at how another country handles teacher training. "Finnish teacher education programs are extremely selective, admitting only one out of every ten students who apply. The result is that Finland recruits from the top quartile of the college-bound cohort" (National Center on Education and the Economy n.d.). The first screening round consists of a review of upper secondary school records and two examinations. "Once an applicant makes it beyond this first screening round, they are then observed in a teaching-like activity and interviewed; only candidates with a clear aptitude for teaching in addition to strong academic performance are admitted" (National Center on Education and the Economy n.d.).

Once admitted to the program, primary school teachers major in education and minor in two school subjects. Secondary school teachers major in the subject they will teach. Fieldwork is a part of the course of study. "Students must also spend a full year teaching in a teacher training school associated with their universities before graduation." These schools "have been particularly designed pedagogically to support both pupils and teacher-students in their learning. They are university-affiliated model schools, where prospective teachers and researchers develop and model new practices and complete research on teaching and learning" (National Center on Education and the Economy n.d.).

It is an interesting footnote that recompense for teachers in Finland is less than in the US and less than the average of many other countries, "but the profession itself is highly regarded and granted a level of respect well above that of teaching in the U.S." Teachers have a high degree of autonomy, having control over their classrooms, lesson plans, and hours outside of teaching. (The article cited above summarizes information from Marc Tucker's book, *Leading High Performance School Systems: Lessons from the World's Best* 2019.)

Let's summarize. The teachers of America are underprepared, underpaid, undervalued, and underrespected for the critical and difficult job they do. Politicians and even school districts malign them. Parents often blame them for their own failings.

A significant percentage of their students have learning or emotional disabilities requiring socioemotional-based instruction at odds with statistical evaluations stressing success on standardized examinations. In 2017–2018, 7 million children or 14% of public school students received special education services under IDEA (National Center for Education Statistics 2019a).

A large number of students are ELLs. In fall of 2016, 4.9 million children or 9.6% of public school students were considered English language learners (National Center for Education Statistics 2019b).

Classrooms are academically, linguistically, racially, and ethnically diverse, requiring culturally responsive teaching and additional teacher time for professional development and individualized lesson planning. Seriously disruptive students, often victims of the deprivations of poverty, face minimal consequences for their actions.

Almost everything regarding teachers, from their university preparation to their first year on the job training to their evaluations, is so poorly done that often our most talented college graduates eschew teaching as a profession or consider it only a temporary step on the career ladder. Let's look at the different aspects of the professional career of a teacher.

Teaching is an honorable profession of service to children and to the future of our democratic ideals. Its purpose has always been to help children become productive members of society, good citizens, good spouses and parents, and competent workers. The definitions of "citizen," "spouses and parents," and "workers" continually change, but this does not alter the fundamental role of teachers.

Given the honorable nature of this profession, why is it that politicians, the press, parents, and even school districts themselves are in attack mode when it comes to teachers? Pick up today's paper. A governor wants more stringent evaluation processes to remove bad teachers. A mayor wants to close a school because all the teachers are not doing their jobs. A parent is suing a teacher and school because her son did not like the tone of the teacher's voice when she critiqued his oral presentation.

Yes, some grievances are true, and some teachers should not be teaching. But maligning an entire profession for the foibles of a small percentage only discourages potentially effective teachers from even considering the profession. What do potential and current teachers want to become and remain educators?

- Salary commensurate with their education and professional responsibilities
- Respect, prestige, and recognition for their work with children
- The ability to use their intelligence, talents, and creativity in their teaching
- Valid evaluations

Salary issues were documented earlier in this chapter. It is a national disgrace that many teachers do not even earn a living wage and that a high percentage need to work second jobs. A mediocre athlete can be paid more money to play one season than a teacher earns in twenty years. For example, a backup major league catcher hitting .161 has earned one million dollars a year.

Stockbrokers and bankers, who profit from the labor of others, earn more in bonuses in one year than most teachers earn in ten. Other professionals with commensurate education, such as nurses, earn considerably more. The starting salary for a nurse with a bachelor's degree is $90,000+ at major New York City hospitals. We expect the best of our teachers, but pay them less than half of what their expertise is worth.

The best and the brightest of our graduates could earn more money as a doctor or lawyer, tech expert, or stockbroker, making teaching a less desirable profession. If teacher salaries were 50% higher, the profession would draw more of these top graduates, particularly those looking for a position that offers the satisfaction of helping others.

In the current economy where many college graduates are underemployed, some teacher salary scales (such as those in the Northeast and on the West Coast) are not totally unattractive, especially if the school system provides good fringe benefits: pension, medical coverage, sick days, and maternity leave. Paradoxically, as the economy improves, more high-paying professional positions are created, and even fewer college graduates will become teachers.

What can we do to recruit and retain the best and the brightest as teachers?

First, restore prestige to the profession. Celebrate and publicize the successes of teachers. Every person reading this book—and every person who ever attended school, including politicians, media reporters, and parents—can point to one or two or many teachers who helped them on their paths to adulthood. Now and then, stories appear about inspirational teachers but only as fillers when there is nothing more newsworthy. For every negative story about a teacher, there should be ten or twenty positive ones. Teachers change the lives of children, of families, and of society itself. We need current and potential teachers to know they are respected for the work they do or will do.

Anyone who has been a teacher has had a relative, friend, or acquaintance comment on how easy teachers have it—working seven hour days and having all those holidays and summers! What a plum job! Most teachers, after trying to explain all the work taken home, all the planning they do on so-called holidays and vacations, just give up because only another teacher really understands what they do. They don't even try to explain the psychological strain of working hour after hour with children who are not yet fully realized persons and with the plethora of other people they have contact with every day: parents, supervisors, aides, custodians, and security guards.

Teaching is one of the last face-to-face people professions. There is no cubicle to hide in, no anonymity of a text, no solitary hours in front of a computer. Everything a teacher does—every lesson planned, every grade labored over, every response to a student paper—affects the life of a child. Teachers need to be proactive and take the time to explain what they do to relatives, friends, and neighbors.

Perhaps we should establish a "take a friend to work" day so that people in other professions and jobs can actually see what teachers do. Of course, they would also have to go home with the teacher and help with the marking of papers and planning for the next day's lessons. They would discover that teachers actually work nearly eleven hours a day (Scholastic n.d.). Maybe after the months of distance learning imposed by the closing of schools during the 2020 pandemic, everyone will have a greater appreciation of the work teachers do.

Second, we need to restore joy and creativity to teaching. The Common Core Learning Standards were meant to provide guidelines to ensure that students across the country mastered the same core of subject matter and were rated by the same standards. These goals have been hampered and perhaps permanently damaged in four ways:

1. The language of the CCLS is obtuse and overly convoluted. The press has had a field day printing some standards written in verbiage a PhD would find hard to understand. The revised versions fail to correct this.
2. As discussed in Chapter 2, departments of education and school districts have taken the CCLS guidelines and infused them with rigid rules, ranging from directed pedagogical methods to providing daily lesson plans to be followed according to a timetable of activities. In some districts, teachers are required to create plans so detailed that they are pages long and impossible to follow while conducting an actual class.
3. Politicians, departments of education, and school districts have allowed curricula to be dictated by publishing companies that create and sell products designed to implement the standards. Once a series of texts is adopted, they become the blueprint for teachers, hindering their creativity.

4. The CCLS are linked to high-stakes testing, for students, teachers, and schools themselves. What was reasonable testing (as at the end of grades five and eight and subject area sequences in high school) has become a yearly grind of pre- and post-testing on ever more grade levels and in more subject areas. This testing has no regard for the reading readiness of the youngest students or the learning styles of older ones. The examination frenzy has turned much of teaching into test preparation and led to a parent revolt. Often, the same educational publishers who create the textbooks create and rate the examinations: the more tests required, the more profit they make.

How do we overcome these obstacles so that teachers will feel they are valued as intelligent, talented, and creative professionals?

We need to go back to seeing the CCLS as guidelines. We need to give teachers freedom to implement them according to the needs of their students and their own teaching styles. We need to greatly reduce testing and make the tests that remain valid evaluations of what we want students to be able to do. If we screen to find the best and the brightest and provide them with appropriate preparation and ongoing in-service support, let's trust them to do their jobs with intelligence, creativity, and joy.

We need to remove ineffective teachers so that they do not besmirch the 99% of teachers who do an effective job. We need to make sure that effective teachers are not unfairly rated. This is a major factor why talented people are not entering teaching and talented teachers are leaving it.

Much is written about how few teachers are rated ineffective and forced to leave teaching, noting almost all teachers seeking tenure after three years of service (or whatever number of years designated by contract) receive it. What the media fail to mention is that 7% of teachers with one to three years of experience leave the profession every year, meaning that about 14% of teachers never even get to their third year (Goldring, Taie, and Riddles 2014, 3). Some teachers are counseled out of the profession or voluntarily leave once it is clear teaching is not the correct career path. Yes, a few principals are not diligent and give less-than-effective teachers tenure, but this is the exception to general practice.

A far more serious problem is the number of good teachers who leave the profession. According the *Washington Post*, "Currently, approximately 8% of teachers leave the profession annually and another 8 percent change schools, creating additional turnover at the school level. . . . Attrition is generally highest in the south and southwest, and lowest in the northeast, where several states have leaving rates under 5%" (Strauss 2017b). This problem is exacerbated by millennial thinking. "Ninety-one percent of Millennials (born between 1977-1997) expect to stay in a job for less than three years" (Meister 2012).

Let's take a mathematical look at teacher turnover. If there is an 8% annual turnover rate and a school has 100 teachers, 8 teachers leave each year. If this applies mainly to new teachers, the school has a revolving door; if it applies across experience levels, there would be a near total staff turnover every twelve years. The reality is probably in between, with well-run schools in safe neighborhoods retaining staff at higher levels than poorly run schools in neighborhoods perceived as dangerous.

Once our college students see teaching as having prestige, we need to convince them to enter the profession. Given the many issues with student loans, a good way to attract college students would be to pay for all or part of their tuition in exchange for five years of teaching service in the public schools. We have the Teaching Fellows and Teach for America, but these programs cover only the cost of the MAT (and, inconceivably, do not require five years of service).

If school districts were to recruit well-qualified candidates after their freshman year in college and offer free tuition to those who enter and successfully complete an undergraduate teacher preparation program, the pool of future teachers would grow exponentially. Unfortunately, this is not a priority for government funding. Just as our shortsighted politicians refuse to address the nation's rising poverty rate and growing income inequality, they fail to see that human investment in potentially competent teachers could be the solution to the worsening teacher shortage.

Schools cannot control the preparation or suitability of teachers who graduate from teacher preparation or alternative programs. They cannot control their states' certification process or requirements. They cannot control their district's screening practices.

They do have near total control over the training provided to newly hired teachers during their critical first year. First-year teachers should be given intensive in-service training, where school supervisors facilitate weekly sessions, provide them with practical pedagogical suggestions, orient them to the culture of the school, and introduce them to key school personnel. General discussions on classroom management, lesson planning, and lesson execution would be followed by one-on-one discussions between the teachers and their immediate supervisors, those who will observe, develop, and evaluate them.

A new teacher should also be paired with a recognized master teacher in the school who is teaching at the same grade level or has the same preps so that they could provide confidential advice and suggestions on a daily basis. In the best of circumstances, the two teachers would have a shortened teaching load or at least a common prep or lunch period so they could confer daily.

Part of this first-year in-service training should be designed to convince teachers to stay in the profession. Much time and effort is being spent to develop effective teachers. It is also costly. "Research shows that teacher replacement costs, including expenses related to separation, recruitment, hiring and training, can range from an average of $9,000 per teacher in rural districts to more than $20,000 in urban districts. A 2007 study estimated a national cost of over $7 billion a year, a price tag that would exceed $8 billion today" (Strauss 2017b).

If staff turn over every few years, this investment is squandered, and the school loses continuity of instruction. New teachers need to learn about their salary scales, medical and pension benefits, life insurance coverage, and union protections. This is easy when there is a living wage with good benefits but is difficult when this is not the case.

The main thrust of this learning curve needs to address the importance of teachers to the lives of their students and their students' families. They need to understand that everything they say and do, from teaching a wonderful lesson to spending five minutes talking to a distraught student to giving words of encouragement, can be the defining moment in the life of a child, helping them become a better person or see the importance of education to achieve a goal. There is no other profession wherein one person can critically affect the lives of so many others. This is both a heavy responsibility and a source of unlimited satisfaction.

Ms. Rayne, the same principal who advised teachers to be a little paranoid, tried to help teachers see the influence they have on the lives of their students. She told her teachers that, if each of them had a major impact on only one student in each class each semester, then over the course of a thirty-year teaching career, each teacher would change the lives of at least 300 students.

That is, 300 students who would go to college and enter well-paying jobs and have children and grandchildren and great grandchildren who follow in their footsteps, ultimately having a positive impact on the lives of thousands for generations to come. Multiply this by the 100 teachers in the school, and the numbers become astronomical. And, she would add, caring teachers positively impact the life of more than one child per class.

(For a more detailed discussion of first-year teacher training, see Chapters 5, 6, and 7 of this author's *Remembering What's Important: Priorities of School Leadership* [2011b].)

In summary, we know that those who enter teacher preparation programs may not be the right people. They may not be teacher material or may not have the appropriate academic background. We know that some colleges do not provide them with good preparation and that the state and local requirements may be substandard. There are severe shortages of teachers in some parts of the country and in certain subject areas. Principals have no control over these facts.

Principals do have a major impact on who they hire and how they train them in their first year and thereafter, but do they make sure that teacher evaluations are done fairly and appropriately? Do current scientific methods of observation discourage new teachers?

Teachers are frustrated by current evaluation methods, often so complicated as to be unintelligible. These methods often force them to arrange their classrooms a certain way, write lengthy lesson plans according to a "suggested" template, and even time each aspect of a lesson.

Scientific metrics for evaluation have become the substitute for the professional development of teachers. Student test results are combined with modern observational systems, such as the use of the Danielson Framework, to rate teachers.

The use of test data is fundamentally flawed since it is statistically suspect to use results from one subject area to rate teachers in others because there are no tests (yet) for physical education, the arts, and some CTE subjects. They are also invalid because teachers are rated by the test results of students they taught in years prior to testing. For example, a kindergarten or first- or second-grade teacher could be rated on the basis of a third-grade test; a sixth-grade teacher, on the basis of an eighth-grade exam; or a ninth-grade teacher, on the basis of a high school exam given in the eleventh or twelfth year. The ignored variables would give a professional statistician apoplexy.

Only 6% of teachers and 23% of parents feel that the percentage of students who pass a test is the best way to measure school performance (Kappaonline.org 2019, K9). Neither is it the best way to measure a teacher's ability.

The use of test scores in teacher evaluations is invalid for many reasons:

- A poor teacher in the testing year could negate the work of previously effective teachers giving them undeserved poor ratings.
- A highly effective teacher in the testing year could mask the poor teaching students received previously giving mediocre or poor teachers good ratings.
- Students mature at different rates due to many factors, only one of which involves schooling. The maturity of the student at the time of the test will affect results.
- Students in more affluent or selective schools tend to do well on examinations, regardless of the instruction they receive. Even poor teachers will do well on this component of teacher evaluations.
- Students in schools in neighborhoods beset by poverty tend to do more poorly on examinations, even with effective teachers who will not score well on this component of teacher evaluations.

This invalid use of test scores is combined with observational evaluations. Using a set of rubrics and descriptors, supervisors rate teachers on a variable number of teaching components, usually using a HEDI-type (highly effective, effective, developing, ineffective) scale. Often, components are rated separately and put into a computerized system that provides a yearly observational rating.

Is there anything new in this? Yes and no. Prior to the implementation of scientific observations, supervisors rated each lesson not as a bunch of components but for the overall effectiveness of the lesson to provide competent instruction. The major practices looked at were the same as those used in the modern frameworks: lesson planning and execution, student engagement, classroom management, student participation and questioning technique, differentiation, and assessment.

Supervisors used judgment, differentiating what they looked for in neophytes, journeymen, and master teachers, fine-tuning the metric used according to the experience of the teacher. First- and second-year teachers are still learning the craft. They did not expect that same level of proficiency from them as they did from a master teacher with five or more years of experience. They did look for the implementation of suggested strategies (now called "next steps") and steady improvement over the first two years.

In the past, supervisors provided teachers with a set of expectations for good teaching. These varied from school to school, district to district, and supervisor to supervisor. Teaching frameworks provide common rubrics and descriptors, known in advance by teachers and their supervisors. As implemented by most school districts, their use ignores the judgment of the supervisors to holistically rate a lesson as good or poor and ignores the experience level of the teachers being observed.

While it could be argued that supervisory expectations may have been idiosyncratic under the old system of evaluation, teaching framework rubrics and descriptors for "ineffective" are so low that a teacher would have to be near comatose to be so rated.

On the other end of the spectrum, some school districts seem to feel that a teacher needs to reach the highly effective level during most observations when framework creators indicate that this is an ideal level rarely attained on an everyday basis.

In summary, while teaching frameworks provide teachers and supervisors with standard rubrics that may look good on paper, several flaws need to be addressed:

- Rubrics need to be appropriate so that "ineffective" is more realistically defined.

- There needs to be some differentiation in the rubrics for teachers at different stages in their development, especially for first- and second-year teachers, so they are not so discouraged that they leave the profession.
- Each lesson needs an overall rating, one that holistically reflects the teaching and learning that took place. A supervisor should be able to determine that a lesson with poor questioning is ineffective, even if other components have higher ratings.
- Districts and supervisors must understand that "highly effective" exists in a rarified atmosphere in which even the best master teachers dwell only part of the time. Having a staff of "effective" teachers is the goal. To use a sports analogy, only a handful of baseball players will hit .300 year after year, so only a few are "highly effective" hitters most of the time. Many will hit .250 and still be effective at the plate.

Finally, frameworks were originally designed as a professional development tool. In our statistical world, this purpose has been forgotten. The emphasis on the use of frameworks needs to be for teacher development, with rating coming into play if the teacher fails to improve.

If we are to retain teachers, we need to provide professional development, not one-size-fits-all rubrics, designed to evaluate rather than train.

If principals can hire the right teachers, provide them with excellent first- and second-year training, and evaluate them fairly (perhaps by finding flexibility in the mandated evaluation metrics), then, regardless of prior preparation, caring and dedicated professionals will be added to the school staff. These teachers will use data to individualize instruction; implement effective classroom procedures; employ interpersonal strategies to help struggling students; and, when necessary, follow referral protocols.

These dedicated teachers will enter classrooms where their students are mesmerized by electronics and uncomfortable with face-to-face interactions. Some of their students will be victims of abuse. Others, due to poverty, will live in neighborhoods that leave them traumatized. Is it any wonder that some will have antisocial tendencies?

New hires and old pros need to address the needs of a constantly evolving student body. This is their responsibility as teachers, just as it is the responsibility of their principals and districts to provide them with the training and tools they will need. Newer teachers were themselves raised in the electronic age and may be better prepared to work with today's children. Their more seasoned colleagues need to become better computer, iPhone, Facebook, and Twitter literate. In the spring of 2020, forced distance learning accelerated the electronic learning curve for many teachers.

Teachers and school-based leaders alike need to learn about mind-elasticity research so they can reach out to students who have suffered abuse and trauma. They need to implement strategies that foster socioemotional learning.

If all this is done, children and schools should do better—within limits. However experienced and caring the teacher, in an elementary school, they are with a child only 20% of the time and then in a class of twenty or twenty-five, which averages out to fourteen or so minutes per child each day. In middle and high schools, with larger class sizes and only a forty-five-minute period, this becomes an average of one minute per day per child.

Some children will find a special connection with some teachers, who will then be able to have a great impact on their lives (perhaps this is Principal Rayne's one child per class). Some children, more adaptable to the classroom setting, will be more susceptible to the instruction and role-modeling of the caring teacher.

For many children, the influence of the 80% of the time at home or with peers will remain the dominant factor for their social, emotional, and psychological well-being, and this will positively or negatively impact their academic success. When this 80% of the time is influenced by poverty, illness, poor parenting, abuse, negative peer pressure, and the other evils of a nation that is not taking care of its own populace, the impact will be decidedly negative.

All teachers deal with classroom management issues, and most will be handled in the classroom with regard for the well-being and self-image of the child. But there are times when one child can disrupt the learning of an entire class; in some cases, a child's actions may go beyond disruption to dangerous. The hands of teachers and principals are often tied in the face of very serious breaches in discipline.

What can we conclude about teachers as a factor in the success of students and schools?

- Teacher turnover and shortages will continue to plague schools without policy changes on the national, state, and local levels. This leads to a lack of continuity for planning and instruction. Better salaries, benefits, and working conditions will improve this situation.
- Candidates entering the teaching profession through traditional and alternative programs are poorly screened and poorly trained. Some will leave after a few years, perpetuating shortages; others may remain providing mediocre instruction.
- Through good hiring practices and professional development programs, particularly in the first and second years, principals can develop caring and dedicated staffs.

- Through creative implementation of evaluation programs, principals can develop staff and demonstrate respect for teachers.
- While dedicated teachers can have a major impact on some students, the influence of parents and peers will dominate the lives of others.
- Even the best teachers may be helpless in the face of societal problems outside the school, particularly low-poverty levels, negatively impacting on the lives of children.
- There is no effective program to address the problems created by students who are unaffected by positive behavioral interventions.

The analytics used to evaluate teacher performance are also questionable. The use of test scores is statistically invalid. "Scientific" observation methods use rubrics created for professional development, not evaluation. The descriptors for "ineffective" are ludicrously low. There is no holistic rating for the effectiveness of the lesson as a whole. The analytics ignore critical variables that impact on student success.

Chapter Eight

Principals

There is an emphasis on the role of the principal (and, by extension, assistant principals and department chairs) as the major factor to set schools on the right track and improve the education of students. There have been sufficient books and articles to support this premise. This chapter accepts that school leadership is critical but overemphasized in an age when principals, having little or no control over the factors discussed in previous chapters, are expected to perform miracles.

Let's begin with terminology. School-based leaders include principals, assistant principals, and department or grade-level chairs. Principals set policies and bear the ultimate responsibility for decisions and actions. Assistant principals and chairs advise the principal, but whether they agree or disagree in private, publicly support and implement the policies set by the school principal within their bailiwicks. Their words and actions reflect the principal's own. In this chapter, we will refer to "the principal" but in doing so include these other leaders, the implementers of school policy.

It is not quite accurate to say that principals set policy. They too are implementers, carrying out the policies of the district, school board, and political entities. Principals are expected to consult with school leadership teams, parents' associations, student governments, teacher teams, and unions when making decisions. They get their "marching orders" from others, who rarely, if ever, consult with them.

Principals operate in straitjackets composed of laws, rules, and regulations; budgetary parameters; school plant design and location; union contracts; national, state, local, and district politics and policies; and the effects of poverty on communities, parents, and children. They are buried under mounds of data and paperwork and have much of their time consumed by disciplinary and legal issues. Their actual decision-making ability and influence are limited.

Let's explore some factors that impact the principalship: turnover, burnout, lack of prestige, a dwindling candidate pool, poor training, and preparation. Then, we will look at what principals can and cannot do.

There is a serious lack of leadership continuity.

> Turnover is a serious issue across the country. The national average tenure of principals in their schools was four years as of 2016–17. This number masks considerable variation, with 35 percent of principals being at their school for less than two years, and only 11 percent of principals being at their school for 10 years or more. The most recent national study of public school principals found that, overall, approximately 18 percent of principals were no longer in the same position one year later. In high-poverty schools, the turnover rate was 21 percent. (Levin and Bradley 2019)

Superville (2018) tells us that "A quarter of the country's principals quit their schools each year, according to the report, and nearly 50 percent leave in their third year." She adds the following:

> Principal turnover is also higher in schools serving larger percentages of students in poverty. In schools where more than 75 percent of students qualified for free and reduced meals, only 79 percent of principals stayed at the same school for the next school year, and 11 percent of them left the principalship altogether. In schools where 34 percent or fewer of the student body qualified for free and reduced meals, 85 percent of principals stayed for the 2016-17 school year.

The COVID-19 pandemic could exacerbate this situation. Nationwide, 27% of principals are over 55 (Will 2020). The course of the virus may determine how many may choose not to return for the next school year.

It takes several years for a newly assigned principal to learn the culture of a school, evaluate personnel, sift through data, develop teams composed of competent and trustworthy educators, and determine a course of action to improve student and school success. It takes additional time for the plan to be fully implemented and results seen: five or six years for elementary schools, two to three years for middle schools, and four years for high schools. One third of principals are gone in two years; the average tenure is four. Is it any wonder that there is little or no change in school and student success rates?

After retiring from the principalship, Ms. Rayne worked part-time for a university teaching educational leadership courses. She facilitated the supervisory internship seminar, the final requirement for teachers seeking state certification. She always gave her students, now beginning to apply for midlevel leadership positons, three pieces of advice:

First, be sure you can have an immediate impact on a school before you apply. You will be expected to solve problems and turn things around the very first year. If you know you cannot do this, don't apply.

Second, to succeed in your position, you need the trust and confidence of your staff. Never treat your staff the way the district and "the powers that be" treat you.

Third, at some time in the future, you will be thinking about becoming a principal. If this is your career goal, wait until you are ten years away from retirement before applying. The principalship gnaws at your time, patience, ability to multitask, and family life. My husband told me that, shortly after becoming a principal, I lost my sense of humor. Ten to twelve years is the maximum length of time the most capable principals are able to handle this immensely complex and difficult job and maintain a semblance of sanity and domestic tranquility.

Why are principals leaving?

> Nearly 30 percent of principals say that they did not have as much enthusiasm for the job now as they did when they first started, and 16 percent say the stress and disappointment are just not worth it. . . . Principals who admitted their enthusiasm for the job had petered out and didn't want to show up for work make up the highest percentage (14 percent) of principals who left the profession, according to the data. Bob Farrace, the spokesman for the National Association of Secondary School Principals, says that given that principals consistently spend more than 60 hours or more weekly on school-related activities, the burnout is not surprising. (Superville 2018)

Let's examine this workload from the perspective of the past four decades. Prior to the 1980s, "the powers that be" sent most information to principals by snail mail (emergency information came via landline telephones because cell phones did not exist). Documents were typed and corrections made using eraser or white-out. Reports due from principals were created the same way. As this was a slow process for all involved, the amount of paper and reports were limited. Principals would usually meet with the superintendent once a month and be given all pertinent documents. They returned to their schools, distributed these materials to the appropriate staff, and then got on with their work of running a school.

By the mid-1980s, "the powers that be" had fax machines. Now, anyone in any office could send documents to schools and ask for immediate fax feedback. The number of documents and required reports increased. But fax machines were in the school, not principals' homes, so there was a beginning and an end to the school day.

Then came the digital age. Almost overnight, districts provided principals with laptops (then tablets) and cell phones so that they would be on call 24/7. Every satrap in any education office could call for an immediate response to whatever document they needed to justify their own position. And the documents sent were not one or two pages. With the correction power of computers, they could be twenty, thirty, or more pages—the longer they were, the more important the satrap felt. Today, for example, in New York City, every principal receives a "Principal's Weekly" email from the chancellor, a document that may run to over forty pages.

In addition, we have noneducator statisticians who create all sorts of documents drawn from mountains of data—all sent to principals for them to sift through and incorporate into one or more of the many required reports and improvement plans. Lest we forget, teachers are also recipients of this overload and told to incorporate data into their plans for individualized instruction (in middle and high schools, for each of thirty children in each of five classes) and creation of peer groupings. If you felt overwhelmed by all the data cited in Chapter 1 of this book, imagine how principals and teachers feel when daily confronted by page after page of data they are told to access and use.

In the 1980s, principals would complain about mounds of paperwork, and in the 1990s, about the number of faxes labeled "Urgent." None of this compares with the petabytes (1000^4) of information and data spewing before, during, and after school hours and on weekends, all demanding immediate response. With all this cyber-madness, is it any wonder principals are burning out?

The numbers do not tell us why the principal turnover rate for schools in high-poverty districts is higher than average. Perhaps the most capable candidates in the pool feel they cannot make an immediate impact on the school and do not apply. Perhaps the schools do not receive the funding needed to support programs for children in need. More likely, in our world, where instant change is expected, superintendents expect a magical turnaround in a short time and remove the principal before they can make an impact. Whatever the reason, poverty has a negative effect on schools, students, and principal longevity.

At the beginning of the 2019 school year, a Pew Research Center study made headlines proclaiming that, of the many professions studied, K–12 principals were the most trusted by Americans, coming in ahead of police officers, military leaders, and religious leaders. At the bottom of the list were local elected officials, journalists, members of Congress, and leaders of tech companies (Pew Research Center 2019).

The news reports were an oversimplification. Let's examine the study more carefully. What is the percentage of US adults who think K–12 public school principals act unethically? Six percent responded "all or most of the time," and 46%, "some of the time." That's over half of the adult population sampled (Pew Research Center 2019, 1).

The report also tried to judge which professions generated the most confidence in Americans. Principals came out on top, but the results were anything but enthusiastic. Forty-five percent of the sampled US adult population felt that principals cared about others or "people like me" all or most of the time—leaving 55% who said some of the time (39%) or none of the time (16%). Only 27% of the surveyed adults felt that principals "provide fair and accurate info to the public" all or most of the time, with 21% indicating "none of the time." Only 29% felt principals "handle resources responsibly" all or most of the time, while 19% said none of the time (Pew Research Center 2019, 3).

Like teachers, the prestige of being a principal—and the trust and confidence in others this leads to—has eroded.

There is a trust problem within schools. School-based leaders are the buffer zone between "the powers that be" and their staffs, explaining and interpreting often conflicting and inconsistent directives to make them more acceptable to staff. Principals walk a tightrope. When a mandate is educationally unsound or unenforceable, principals cannot directly say so without risking censure from their districts. Neither can they sell it to their staffs as written without losing personal trust in their leadership abilities.

The most successful school-based leaders walk this tightrope well, but, as time goes on, the rope and the principal's state of mind become more frayed. It is difficult to spend time and effort and not be able to say the truth directly. Ms. Rayne was thinking about this when she said that ten to twelve years is the maximum time a principal can last.

Principals are also in a frustrating position when it comes to contract negotiations with districts and localities. Teachers can and will, if necessary, go on strike to gain benefits, such as salary increases and/or better schools for children, such as the demand for a nurse in every school in the 2019 Chicago teacher strike.

Negotiators for districts and localities know that school-based leaders will not strike. Principals worry about what will happen to their schools and students. They know that schools will continue to operate, albeit sans leadership, without them in the building. Districts publicly tout the importance of principals, the difficulty of their jobs, and the immensity of their responsibility while at the same time denying contractual demands that would improve schools, lessen paperwork, or raise salaries to appropriate levels.

Let's take a brief foray into principals' salaries. The median salary for a principal in the US is $106,932. Nationwide, 10% of principals earn $83,085 or less, and 10% earn $132,459 or more. Regions, states, and districts display a wide range of variation. The median salary in Mississippi is $93,031, with 10% earning $115,239 or more; the median salary in California is $119,443 with 10% earning $147,956 or more (Salary.com 2020). Walmart store managers in the US make an average of $175,000 per year. The qualifications listed for a manager in Dearborn, Michigan, included "a bachelor's degree and two years of general management experience or, without a degree, four years of general management experience" (Berger 2019, 2–3). The average principal salary in Dearborn is $109,563 (Salary.com 2020).

When it comes to contract negotiations, "the powers that be" show no respect for the very school leaders they praise for the work they do. They do not provide salaries commensurate with their academic degrees, years of teaching, midlevel supervisory experience, responsibility for the safety and education of hundreds or even thousands of students, the supervision of scores of staff, and the administration of a multimillion-dollar school budget.

Another important factor relating to the principalship is the dwindling number of competent educators seeking leadership positons. A MetLife survey found that 84% of teachers "were either 'not very' or 'not at all' interested in becoming a principal" (Riggs 2013). How can we convince the best educators to become school leaders?

In the not too distant past, a talented college graduate entering the profession looked toward a career ladder that would include being a master teacher, then a chair or assistant principal, and then a principal within the first ten to fifteen years of their professional lives. This is no longer the case.

As noted in the previous chapter, it is difficult to convince graduates to become educators in the first place, as seen by a dramatic decrease in enrollment in schools of education. If they do become teachers, many do not see education as a lifelong career with opportunities for advancement but rather as one phase of their working lives that will lead to careers in different fields. Those who do see education as their vocation rarely aspire to leave the classroom.

There are several reasons for this:

First, master teachers clearly see the jobs of school leaders as having more to do with administration, investigation, and public relations than with education. Ask intermediate supervisors what percentage of their day is devoted to staff development (including the observation process) and curriculum writing, and you will find it compares poorly to the time spent analyzing data;

completing reports; disciplining students; meeting with parents; attending meetings; and handling allegations of bullying, harassment, and verbal abuse.

This is less likely to happen in large schools where there are designated assistant principals of guidance, administration, security, and/or technology, allowing grade-level or subject-specific chairs to focus more on teaching and learning. But, as the trend toward boutique schools continues, the number of intermediate supervisors in the school decreases, and those who remain become generalists with multiple responsibilities.

Second, teachers see school leaders as being more and more divorced from teaching and learning, the very reason they became educators. They simply prefer working with students to working with all the adult constituencies inside and outside of the school.

Third, the time demands on school leaders are far greater than on classroom teachers. Often, they are expected to arrive early and leave late, to attend school and community events, and be on call 24/7. Master teachers spend time writing lesson plans, correcting papers, and working one-on-one with students, but the job does not involve sacrificing their personal lives. In our current corporate model of education, assistant principals and principals are department managers and CEOs. They are always on call but without the prestige and salaries of their corporate peers, even though they have the far more important task of preparing children for college, career, and life.

Finally, the salary differential between a master teacher with ten years or more experience and a newly assigned intermediate school-based leader is relatively small, so there is little monetary motivation to take on the demands of school leadership.

As a result, sometimes those filling leadership positions find themselves settling for the best of a pool of less-than-the-best candidates. The most able and dedicated professionals prefer to remain with their students in the classroom.

What can be done to remedy this situation?

In our politically established factory model, principals are now managers of schools, not educators. Some school systems take academically able teachers from prestigious universities and enroll them in principal training programs after one or two years of teaching. These young lions are then put into difficult schools and expected to turn them around in one year. Most fail.

In Great Britain, schools are led by headmasters (i.e., master teachers). The head of school is first and foremost a recognized educator with many years of teaching experience, making them able to communicate well with colleagues, parents, students, and superiors. These are critical attributes for a principal. There needs to be managerial expertise, but a manager who does not understand good teaching and learning will make poor decisions for a school. Likewise, a school leader lacking tact, political savvy, and team building expertise will falter.

Modern thinking seems to indicate that traditional university schools of education have failed to produce effective school leaders (and teachers); therefore, districts and state lawmakers have created alternate paths to the principalship, as expensive district-designed preparation programs. These have led to even more poorly prepared school leaders because the method of candidate selection has more to do with academic prowess than supervisory, people, and administrative skills.

There are several steps that need to be taken to ensure the competency of teachers seeking supervisory certification either through a university or district-based program.

First, candidates for assistant principalships or chairs must be master teachers. A minimum of five years of successful teaching should be required before a candidate enters a program, university, or alternative.

Second, as part of the application process, candidates should be expected to provide evidence of their professionalism: service in quasi-supervisory roles as programmer, dean, focus group, and curriculum leader; volunteering to present at department meetings, parent association meetings, and district forums; and verification of exemplary service to the needs of students beyond regular teaching hours (before and after-school tutoring with or without extra pay). Sadly, too many candidates for higher positions do so to seek power, not realizing that the role of the school leader is one of service.

Third, as part of the application process, candidates should be expected to provide at least two letters of recommendation written by school supervisors attesting that they have demonstrated supervisory, administrative, and people skills, citing solid contributions to the school community.

Fourth, the candidate needs to provide on-demand written documents that demonstrate effective written communication skills. The average school leader routinely writes reports, plans, observations, curriculum guides, recommendations, and letters, all of which are expected to be of the highest professional quality.

Fifth, candidates entering a certification program need to have the face-to-face people skills necessary for success. An in-depth interview could help a university or alternative program determine this intangible. Such interviews are standard when certified school leaders seek supervisory positions. They should be required at the entry stage of the program so that applicants do not waste time and money seeking a position for which they might not have the temperament. University and district legal experts will need to be consulted to be sure the process is fair and equitable.

Sixth, we need to create a preparation program that balances theory and practice, having certification candidates intern in schools and receive instruction from both college professors and practicing school leaders. (For further details, see Chapter 3 of *Becoming a School Leader* [Bonnici 2014].)

Finally, the initial leadership position should be that of assistant principal or chair. Only after successful completion of at least five years in this position should a candidate be able to apply for a principalship.

Ms. Rayne had seven assistant principals in her high school of 1,800 students. As she approached retirement, she realized that five of these APs also would be retiring just before or after herself.

She wanted to encourage her best teachers to seek supervisory certification so they could replace those retiring, providing leadership continuity for the school. She invited her best and brightest to an informal meeting. It soon became apparent that these master teachers preferred to remain in the classroom.

Ms. Rayne had an inspiration. She explained that as teachers they had impact on the lives of about 150 students per year. As an AP, they would have impact on far more students. Their expertise would be part of their training of the teachers they supervised, impacting indirectly on the education of the 1,800 students in the school. This influence would continue into the next generation, as some of the teachers they hired and trained would, in turn, become APs training more teachers and future APs.

She added that knowing the school and its students would give them a shorter supervisory learning curve. In addition, they would have more loyalty to the students and vision of the school than an outside applicant.

Several continued to attend weekly meetings as part of a teacher-to-assistant principal program; they obtained their certifications. Five years after her retirement, most of the AP positions in Ms. Rayne's school were filled by the teachers who attended that first informal meeting.

Let's say we do find ways to encourage the best and the brightest to become school leaders. Let's say we provide them with an educational program that combines theory with practice and that upon earning certification they find a supervisory position. How do we reduce turnover in the first few years?

A new principal enters a school that probably has one or more serious issues. This principal has had no input into the staff, not even any assistant principals or chairs who may be in the school. The budget for the school year was probably created by the previous principal or an assigned administrator from the district. This principal is told that major improvements are expected by the end of the school year. Unless the new principal has the charisma of a Martin Luther King and the corporate expertise of a Bill Gates, this is not going to happen.

A competent neophyte can make administrative changes that will lead to some immediate improvement, but changing the culture of a school takes time. A first step, often neglected, is that the new school leader needs to get to know the staff—capabilities, strengths, and weaknesses. They also need to know the other key players—teachers, parents, and student leaders; the superintendent and district administrators; community organizations; and local businesses. The larger the school, the longer this will take.

Once the principal gains this knowledge, he or she can orchestrate the constituencies to create a viable vision for the school. Then, strategies need to be determined and implemented to improve instruction and better meet student needs. This will include curriculum modifications and intensive staff development. The strategies need to be evaluated and reassessed as needed. Finally, systems must be put in place so that the changes become part of the fabric of the school.

What can be done to support and encourage new school leaders?

First, school district leaders need to have realistic expectations regarding what a neophyte principal can accomplish. These expectations need to be individualized for each school. The district superintendent should work with the current leadership team, staff, and parents (and on the middle and high school levels, students) to determine a preliminary plan and time frame for improvement, later to be modified by input from the newly assigned principal. The time frame must allow for at least three years for major aspects of the improvement plan to be accomplished. Likewise, principals must have realistic expectations for newly assigned assistant principals and chairs, providing them with similar supports.

Second, these same districts need to provide newly assigned school leaders with ongoing staff development that addresses their needs and ensures they have a firm grasp of: contractual matters; budgets; school programming; legal matters, including investigatory procedures and federal and state education laws; effective observation and staff development techniques; and time management strategies. Much of this can be done over the summer to minimize the number of times new principals are required to be out of their buildings.

Third, keeping in mind that superintendents change every three to five years, there must be a district continuity plan in place so that school leaders are not subject to the changing visions of newly assigned superintendents within the time frames they have been given.

More needs to be done to encourage all principals to remain for longer periods of time.

First, recognize that principals have spouses and children of their own, and give them back their lives. There should be no emails, texts, or phone calls after 6:00 p.m. each day and none on weekends, holidays, or vacations.

Period. No exceptions. If you were to say "only in emergencies," everyone in the district will say every contact is an emergency. No it isn't. It can wait until the morning of the next school day.

Second, end the cyber-madness. Greatly reduce the documents sent and feedback required and eliminate duplication in the paperwork. Obtain data centrally from the district data base, rather than ask the principal to do it (and get the data right so that a principal does not need to spend hours correcting it). If the district wants principals to be instructional leaders, then give them the time to lead.

Third, remove the responsibility for investigations from the principal. Modify policies that the school has neither the personnel nor expertise to address, such as making schools responsible for monitoring student electronic communications outside the campus. If needed, create the district-funded position of "on-site investigator" in each school to address the never-ending allegations of bullying, verbal and physical abuse, and teacher misconduct.

Fourth, allow principals and teachers to make curricula decisions, instead of dictating how policies, such as the Common Core, will be implemented.

Fifth, provide sufficient funding and personnel to address the ever-increasing number of English language learners and students with special needs. Perhaps each school should have an assigned compliance specialist who will be take responsibility for making sure all students receive the required supports.

Sixth, create district-wide policies to address the problem of the small percentage of students for whom restorative justice and other positive disciplinary strategies have failed and who prey on other students and disrupt classrooms. This will not be easy since every child is entitled to a free, appropriate public education. At the same time, a few students should not be allowed to disrupt the education of the rest of the school. Maybe distance or blended learning could provide a solution.

We also need to look beyond school administration, data, and analytics. We need to ensure our school leaders have people skills.

Almost all current school-based leader training deals with school management, data-driven instruction, and the use of statistics to improve schools. True leadership depends more on the art of establishing positive relationships with all constituencies. Good outcomes depend on the ambience of the school, a direct result of the leadership style of its principal and assistant principals.

If the screening and selection processes discussed above are successful, the new school leader would begin as a

- capable manager who pays attention to details;
- highly effective and respected teacher and lifelong learner;

- professional able to establish positive relations with students, parents, colleagues, and supervisors;
- competent oral and written communicator.

Most newly assigned school leaders are provided with ongoing training and support in all aspects of school management and administration but not in the crucial socioemotional dimension. This may best be provided through well-designed individualized coaching and peer-group conversations centered on the development of personalized, effective leadership styles that promote optimal interpersonal relations. Possible topics could include (the following is adapted from *Creating a Successful Leadership Style* [Bonnici 2011a]):

- The importance of being a role model. What school leaders say is less important than what they do. Principals and assistant principals who issue directives from their offices are less effective than those who are visible and doing.
- School leaders know how to defuse potentially volatile situations, rather than exacerbate them. School leaders who maintain composure amidst chaos, allow others to vent, and then seek calm resolution succeed better than those who join the fray.
- Successful leaders listen more than they speak. In a world where everyone is electronically plugged in to everyone else, it is ironic how few people actually listen to each other. School leaders who listen, take notes on what others say, and then address the matter or solve the problem will succeed far better than those who dominate the conversation.
- School leaders do not promote themselves. Instead, they give credit to staff, students, and parents as much as possible. School leaders make policies and devise procedures. Nothing happens unless they are implemented by staff and accepted by students and parents.
- When something goes wrong, school leaders should take the blame. They will not blame others for school issues or give excuses to "the powers that be." They will accept responsibility and then be proactive, providing plans to remedy situations before they are even requested. School leaders who say "I am sorry" gain respect and defuse problems.
- Even if districts reduce paper and cyber work, a principal will still have mounds of real and electronic paper to get through each day. A school is a people place. People, not paper, need to be the priority at all times. A school leader devises systems to complete paperwork efficiently to create more time for interactions with staff, students, and parents.
- Successful principals and assistant principals share leadership, delegating tasks to appropriate personnel. They do not micromanage nor redo

the work others do for them. They learn to train others to complete tasks appropriately and accept competency rather than perfection. They know which tasks should be handled personally. The positives of empowering the professional staff far outweigh the problems caused by occasional lapses in the judgment of those so empowered.
- A common complaint of teachers is that supervisors forget what it was like to be in a classroom. The creation of a school's program, for example, is an administrative puzzle with a multitude of variables to vex school leaders. To teachers, however, programs determine their professional happiness for the year. Their need for particular time schedules or certain classes or even desired rooms must be part of the equation. The well-being of people affected by decisions is more important than an abstract perfect solution.
- Good decisions and policies come not by fiat, but by laying the groundwork and meeting with those involved one-on-one. Effective school leaders will speak with those most affected by a decision, modify ideas based on these conversations, and determine the acceptable level of support needed for implementation. By the time school leaders introduce a plan or policy to the appropriate constituency, they will already have the support needed for its approval without undue dissension.
- Even in the best schools, there is staff turnover. This should not come as a surprise to the school leader who will implement strategies, especially regarding the replacement of key personnel. They will identify needs before they occur (such as knowing when a dean or assistant principal plans to retire) and then train appropriate personnel as replacements before they actually assume the positions.
- School leaders know that all staff members have pluses and minuses. The teacher who gets excellent results with an AP class may have classroom discipline issues with incoming students. The school technology expert may understand computers better than people. In our disposable world, it seems that teachers have become objects to discontinue, rather than people to train. Principals and assistant principals must continually train staff, find and exploit their talents to best support the students, and then address their weaknesses to minimize their impact on students and the school community.
- We live in a world of websites, tweets, and snap chats. A negative viral video can undo years of hard work. School leaders must be sure that all communication from them or any staff member reflects positively on the school. The school must develop communication and technology protocols, based on district policies and guidelines. Students and staff must receive instruction in the appropriate use and dangers of technology. School leaders will be cognizant of recent court decisions regarding school and student communications.

- The school leader pays attention to what may seem trivial details. The theory of chaos can be applied to a school. A minor issue during the first period becomes a crisis by the end of the day. While not micromanaging, successful principals pay attention to the minutia of running a school. They create policies so that a parent is seen in a timely fashion; teachers can easily duplicate instructional materials; or a student needing a program change receives one quickly.
- Many training programs for school leaders tell them to think outside the box. This can be problematic. The "box" is often made up of the walls of state, federal, and district rules and regulations as well as provisions of the multiple contracts of staff members. To think outside this box is to risk reprimand or even dismissal. Successful school leaders learn to maneuver within the box and stretch its sides. A brilliant plan that ignores the box and succeeds will bring accolades. If the same plan fails, the school leader will be back in the classroom. Principals need to understand that life is unfair.
- The school leader always needs to remember what's important. New principals and assistant principals can be distracted by so much these days: statistics, new curricula mandates, revised federal regulations, national and local politics that impact education, interdepartmental or intergrade squabbles, personality conflicts, paper, emails, and tweets. It's easy to forget their real job and the job of everyone in the school: to serve the needs of its clients—the students and their parents. School leaders who always remember their true jobs when completing whatever task can never go wrong.

Newly assigned school leaders can help themselves in two ways.

First, they should join and seek help from professional organizations, whether local, statewide, or national. This could be through informal outreach or by taking advantage of professional development opportunities.

Second, they should create their own networks of support with other supervisors in similar positions in similar schools. This could take the form of phone calls or emails for help and advice or informal meetings, face-to-face or remote, to discuss problems and issues. New school leaders often feel alone, overwhelmed by a myriad of seemingly unique problems. They need to network with others who face similar problems to learn they are not alone and that together they can find solutions.

Let's suppose that competent college students enter the teaching profession and after becoming master teachers aspire to school-based leadership positions. Both as teachers and school leaders they will enter a world where the analytics used to determine student and school success are invalid, as are the methods used to evaluate their own effectiveness. These analytics fail to take into account the other factors discussed in this book, as summarized in Table 8.1.

Table 8.1. Extent of a Principal's Control over Factors Influencing a School's Success

Factor	Extent of the Principal's Control
Poverty and Income Inequality	No control.
School Allocations	Negligible control over the allocations of funds received. Principals can lobby for more money and seek grants from nonprofits. Lobbying will likely fail; grants will help. Both will take staff time and effort to implement and assess.
Federal Monies Allocated for Social Programs and Education	No control.
Policy and Curriculum Mandates	No control. Principals are obligated to implement these mandates, often without additional funding.
Lack of Continuity of Vision from the District and Frequent Changes in Policies	No control. On the positive side, veteran teachers and principals know that good teaching is good teaching regardless of this year's emphasis. On the negative side, effective new strategies may be ignored as just another innovation that will be passé the next year.
National Policies Relating to School Safety, Charter Schools, and Home Instruction	No control. These policies reduce the budget, such as to pay for additional security personnel in an age of gun violence; reduce space, flexibility, and ambience, such as in the case of shared buildings with charter schools; and reduce funding, such as when children are homeschooled.
School Location and Design	Negligible control. Depending on capacity flexibility, available funds, and the supporting walls of the structure, some design modifications may be possible.
School Facilities	No control. Capital budgets are determined by districts and politicians. The principal can only request upgrades.
Inadequate Space and Shared Space Limitations	Negligible control. In shared spaces, principals can meet to make equitable use of facilities.
Parenting	No control over the first and most formative years of a child's life. No control over the 80% of a child's waking hours when not in school. Principals can work with caring parents to help children.
Effects of Poverty on Children	Negligible control. Growth mindset strategies provide help for some students, but sometimes the effects of poverty negatively affect students' ability to succeed in school and in life.

(continued)

Table 8.1. *Continued*

Factor	Extent of the Principal's Control
Students and Technology	No control over technology and social media outside of the school.
	Schools are often expected to address inappropriate emails and cyberbullying that occur off campus without the time, technical skills, or police power needed to do so.
Consistently Disruptive and Dangerous Students	Some control.
	Principals can implement PBIS, restorative justice, and other positive interventions to deal with disruptive behavior. Support resources may be concentrated on 5% of the student population to the detriment of the other 95%.
	When positive interventions fail, principals have few options to keep disruptive students in check and protect the majority of the student body.
School Support Staff	Some control.
	Principals inherit the support staff, many of whom have worked in the school a long time and make up the underlying bureaucracy.
	Principals have considerable control over the organization, assignment, training, and supervision of most of the support staff. It will take the principal time and effort to learn the abilities of each staff member, create job descriptions, match personnel to jobs, and provide training.
	The principal usually has no control over the hiring of school security guards. Through consultation with the hiring agency (district or local police department), they may be able to have a say in security guard training and better integrate them into the school's security team.
Contracts	No control.
	Principals usually have no input into the contracts negotiated for teachers, secretaries, school aides, custodians, etc.
	While contract provisions may improve working conditions for staff, they often lead to additional costs not covered by the district and/or a lessening of flexibility of school schedules, programming, etc.
Teacher Preparation Programs	No control.
Teacher Salaries	No control.
	Principals can make teachers aware of benefits and the important work they do with children.

Factor	Extent of the Principal's Control
Teacher Training and Evaluation	A great deal of control. Principals can find flexibility in the statistical and evaluative methods used to provide positive feedback to teachers and to help first- and second-year teachers improve without causing discouragement.
Creating a Positive School Ambience by Knowing the Constituencies, Building Consensus, and Creating a Vision	Total control. The leadership style of the principal is critical in building trust, fostering consensus, and creating a team of dedicated professionals and support staff. Too often, a principal does all the right things but is not given the time to change the culture of the school.

The statisticians will continue to ignore these factors and rate schools and educators on test scores. Competent principals will not be given the time to have a real impact before the numbers say they should be removed. Teachers see this happen and will not aspire to be school-based leaders.

Let's assume we are in Utopia. "The powers that be" have statisticians create analytics that incorporate *all* the factors impacting on children. They will find that many of the most successful schools and principals do well because of factors outside the school, related to the lack of poverty and income inequality in the school or district area. They will find that some of the least successful schools do not improve not because of poor efforts by principals and staff but because of the effects of these same factors.

What is needed? A total shift in national economic policies to eliminate gross poverty and income inequality in the richest nation in the world. If we combine this with the suggestions for improvement made in this book, the US will have a world-class school system where the vast majority of children and schools succeed. Without such a policy shift, our country will have a mediocre system where poverty and income inequality are perpetuated, where the children of the rich achieve more school success than children of the poor, deepening the gap between have and have-nots and propelling it forward into future generations.

Bibliography

Agreement between Board of Education Wyandanch Union Free School District and Wyandanch Teachers' Association, July 1, 2016–June 30, 2022.

Agreement between the Syosset Central School District, County of Nassau, Syosset, New York and the Syosset Teachers Association, July 1, 2017–June 30, 2020. https://www.syossetschools.org/site/handlers/filedownload.ashx?moduleinstanceid=832&dataid=9296&FileName=Syosset_Teachers_Assoc.pdf.

Alcorn, Chauncey. 2020. "Gun Sales Surge as Coronavirus Pandemic Spreads." *CNN Business*. Updated March 19, 2020. https://www.cnn.com/2020/03/19/business/coronavirus-gun-sales/index.html.

Alexander, Debbie, and Laurie Lewis. 2014. *Condition of America's Public School Facilities: 2012–13*. National Center for Education Statistics, United States Department of Education. https://nces.ed.gov/pubs2014/2014022.pdf.

American Association of School Administrators. 2006. "Superintendent and District Data." https://www.aasa.org/content.aspx?id=740.

American School Counselor Association. n.d. "Student-to-School-Counselor Ratio 2017-2018." https://www.schoolcounselor.org/asca/media/asca/home/Ratios17-18.pdf.

American Society for the Positive Care of Children. 2018. "Child Maltreatment Statistics in the U.S." https://americanspcc.org/child-abuse-statistics/.

AngloInfo. n.d. "Find Out about the Leave and Benefit Entitlements for Parents in Mexico." https://www.angloinfo.com/how-to/mexico/healthcare/pregnancy-birth/maternity-rights.

Associated Press. 2020. "School Shutdowns Raise Stakes of Digital Divide for Students." *Chicago Sun Times*, March 30, 2020. https://chicago.suntimes.com/coronavirus/2020/3/30/21199809/school-shutdowns-digital-divide-students-coronavirus-covid-19-learning-at-home.

Bassuk, Ellen L., Carmela J. DeCandia, Corey Ann Beach, and Fred Berman. 2014. *America's Youngest Outcasts: A Report Card on Child Homelessness*. https://www

.air.org/sites/default/files/downloads/report/Americas-Youngest-Outcasts-Child-Homelessness-Nov2014.pdf.

Berger, Sarah. 2019. "Walmart Says Its US Store Managers Make an Average of $175,000 Per Year." *CNBC*. Published May 9, 2019. https://www.cnbc.com/2019/05/09/walmart-report-reveals-average-salary-of-its-us-store-managers.html.

Betancourt, Sarah. 2018. "Teacher Shortages Worsening in the Majority of US States, Study Reveals." *The Guardian*, September 6, 2018. https://www.theguardian.com/us-news/2018/sep/06/teacher-shortages-guardian-survey-schools.

Bonnici, Charles A. 2011a. *Creating a Successful Leadership Style: Principles of Personal Strategic Planning*. Lanham, MD: Rowman & Littlefield.

Bonnici, Charles A. 2011b. *Remembering What's Important: Priorities of School Leaders*. Lanham, MD: Rowman & Littlefield.

Bonnici, Charles A. 2014. *Becoming a School Leader: Application, Interviews, Examinations and Portfolios*. Lanham, MD: Rowman & Littlefield.

Boyd, Don, Hamp Lankford, Susanna Loeb, Matt Ronfeldt, and Jim Wyckoff. 2010. "The Effect of School Neighborhoods on Teacher Career Decisions." Paper prepared for the conference *New Evidence on How Families, Neighborhoods and Labor Affect Educational Opportunities for American Children*, September 24–25, Brookings, Washington, DC. https://cepa.stanford.edu/sites/default/files/Neighborhoods%2006Jan2010.pdf.

"Broad Discontent Leads Half of Teachers to Consider Quitting Their Jobs." 2019. 51st Annual PDK Poll. *Phi Delta Kappan* 101, no. 1 (September): K3–K5.

Bui, Quoctrung, and Claire Cain Miller. 2018. "The Age That Women Have Babies: How a Gap Divides America. *New York Times*, August 4, 2018. https://www.nytimes.com/interactive/2018/08/04/upshot/up-birth-age-gap.html

Calm Every Storm Crises Consultant Group. n.d. "Gang Violence in Schools—5 Facts You Didn't Know." https://www.crisisconsultantgroup.com/school-violence-prevention/gang-violence-in-schools/.

Camera, Lauren. 2017. "U.S. Trails in Early Childhood Education Enrollment." *U.S. News and World Report*, June 21, 2017. https://www.usnews.com/news/best-countries/articles/2017-06-21/us-falls-behind-other-developed-countries-in-early-childhood-education-enrollment.

Centers for Disease Control and Prevention. 2013. "Asthma-related Missed School Days among Children aged 5–17 Years." Modified October 5, 2015. https://www.cdc.gov/asthma/asthma_stats/missing_days.htm.

"Child Abuse Statistics and Facts." 2014. *Childhelp*. https://www.childhelp.org/child-abuse-statistics/.

"Child Maltreatment 2017." 2019. Children's Bureau, U.S. Department of Health and Human Services. https://www.acf.hhs.gov/cb/resource/child-maltreatment-2017.

Citizens Budget Commission. 2017. "New York per Pupil Education Spending Is Nation's Highest: Where Does the Money Come From?" Published September 7, 2017. https://cbcny.org/research/new-york-pupil-education-spending-nations-highest.

Coalition for Responsible Home Education. n.d. "Homeschooling: The Research." https://responsiblehomeschooling.org/research/.

Coleman-Jensen, Alisha, Matthew P. Rabbitt, Christian A. Gregory, and Anita Singh. 2019. "Household Food Security in the United States in 2018." U.S. Department of Agriculture, Economic Research Service. https://www.ers.usda.gov/publications/pub-details/?pubid=94848.

Danielson, Charlotte. 2007. *Enhancing Professional Practice: A Framework for Teaching (Professional Development)*. Alexandria, VA: ASCD.

DeSilver, Drew, Michael Lipka, and Dalia Fahmy. 2020. "10 Things We Know about Race and Policing in the U.S." *Pew Research Center*. Published June 3, 2020. https://www.pewresearch.org/fact-tank/2020/06/03/10-things-we-know-about-race-and-policing-in-the-u-s/.

Donaldson, Morgaen L., and Susan Moore. 2011. "TFA Teachers: How Long Do They Teach? Why Do They Leave?" *Education Week*. Published October 4, 2011. https://www.edweek.org/ew/articles/2011/10/04/kappan_donaldson.html.

DoSomething.org. 2014. "11 Facts about Teens and Drug Use." https://www.dosomething.org/us/facts/11-facts-about-teens-and-drug-use.

Eckenrode, John, Elliott G. Smith, Margaret E. McCarthy, and Michael Dineen. 2014. "Income Inequality and Child Maltreatment in the United States." *Pediatrics* 133, no. 3 (March): 454–61. https://doi.org/10.1542/peds.2013-1707.

Editorial Board. 2020. "Locked Out of the Virtual Classroom." *New York Times*, March 27 2020. https://www.nytimes.com/2020/03/27/opinion/coronavirus-internet-schools-learning.html.

Education Commission of the States. 2018. "50-State Comparison: Does the State Have Any Caps on the Number of Charter Schools?" http://ecs.force.com/mbdata/mbquestNB2C?rep=CS1703.

Education Commission of the States. 2019. "50-State Comparison: K–12 School Safety." https://www.ecs.org/50-state-comparison-k-12-school-safety/.

Education Commission of the States. 2020. "50-State Comparison: Charter School Policies." Published January 28, 2020. https://www.ecs.org/charter-school-policies/.

Filardo, M., J. M. Vincent, and K. Sullivan. 2019. "How Crumbling School Facilities Perpetuate Inequality." *Phi Delta Kappan* 100, no. 9 (May): 27–31.

Fontenot, Kayla, Jessica Semega, and Melissa Kollar. 2018. "Income and Poverty in the United States: 2017." *U.S. Census Bureau*. Published September 2018. https://www.census.gov/library/publications/2018/demo/p60-263.html.

Fordham University. n.d. "Privacy Education." https://www.fordham.edu/info/24071/privacy_education.

Fulghum, Robert. 1986. *All I Really Need to Know I Learned in Kindergarten*. New York: Ivy Books.

Governing.com. 2016. "Education Spending Per Student by State." Updated June 1, 2018. https://www.governing.com/gov-data/education-data/state-education-spending-per-pupil-data.html.

Kappaonline.org. 2019. "Frustration in the Schools: Teachers Speak Out on Pay, Funding, and Feeling Valued." Published September 2019. https://www.kappanonline.org/wp-content/uploads/2019/08/pdk_101_1_PollSupplement.pdf.

Goldring, R., S. Taie, and M. Riddles. 2014. *Teacher Attrition and Mobility: Results From the 2012–13 Teacher Follow-up Survey.* National Center for Education Statistics. https://nces.ed.gov/pubs2014/2014077.pdf.

Goldstein, Dana. 2014. *The Teacher Wars: A History of America's Most Embattled Profession.* New York: Anchor.

Gramlich, John, and Katherine Schaeffer. 2019. "7 Facts About Guns in U.S." *Pew Research Center.* Published October 22, 2019. https://www.pewresearch.org/fact-tank/2019/10/22/facts-about-guns-in-united-states/.

Hair, Nicole L., Jamie L. Hanson, Barbara L. Wolfe, and Seth D. Pollak. 2015. "Association of Child Poverty, Brain Development, and Academic Achievement." *JAMA Pediatrics* 169, no. 9: abstract. https://doi.org/10.1001/jamapediatrics.2015.1475.

Hancock, Lynnell. 2011. "A+ for Finland." *Smithsonian* 42, no. 5 (September): 94.

Hayasaki, Ericka. 2016. "How Poverty Affects the Brain." *Newsweek.* Published August 25, 2016. https://www.newsweek.com/2016/09/02/how-poverty-affects-brains-493239.html.

Home School Legal Defense Association (HSLDA). n.d. "Home School Laws by State." https://hslda.org/legal/.

Hudespeth, Mark, producer. 2019. "A Real Education: How We Have Failed Our Teachers." *CBS News Sunday Morning.* Updated September 15, 2019. https://www.cbsnews.com/news/how-we-have-failed-our-teachers/.

Huffington Post Canada. 2012. "Maternity Leaves Around the World: Worst and Best Countries for Paid Maternity Leave." Updated November 18, 2015. https://www.huffingtonpost.ca/2012/05/22/maternity-leaves-around-the-world_n_1536120.html.

Izard, Ernest. 2016. *Teaching Children from Poverty and Trauma.* National Education Association. Published June 2016. http://www.nea.org/assets/docs/20200_Poverty%20Handbook_flat.pdf.

Just Think Twice. n.d. "How Does Drug Use Affect Your High School Grades?" https://www.justthinktwice.gov/how-does-drug-use-affect-your-high-school-grades.

Larson, Erik. 2020. "NRA Sues New York State Governor Over Closure of Gun Stores." *Bloomberg.* Published April 3, 2020. https://www.yahoo.com/news/nra-sues-york-state-governor-011213287.html.

Laughlin, Lynda. 2013. "Who's Minding the Kids? Child Care Arrangements: Spring 2011." *U.S. Census Bureau.* Published April 2013. https://www.census.gov/prod/2013pubs/p70-135.pdf.

Leachman, Michael. 2018. "K-12 Funding Cuts Include Capital Spending to Build and Renovate Schools." *Center on Budget and Policy Priorities.* Published June 25, 2018. https://www.cbpp.org/blog/k-12-funding-cuts-include-capital-spending-to-build-and-renovate-schools.

Levin, Stephanie, and Kathryn Bradley. 2019. "Understanding and Addressing Principal Turnover: A Review of the Research." *Learning Policy Institute.* Published March 19, 2019. https://learningpolicyinstitute.org/product/nassp-understanding-addressing-principal-turnover-review-research-report.

MacKay, Kerri. 2016. "Children, Asthma and Poverty: The Facts." *Asthma.net.* Published December 21, 2016. https://asthma.net/living/children-and-poverty-the-facts/.

Meister, Jeanne. 2012. "The Future of Work: Job Hopping Is the 'New Normal' for Millennials." *Forbes*. Published August 14, 2012. https://www.forbes.com/sites/jeannemeister/2012/08/14/the-future-of-work-job-hopping-is-the-new-normal-for-millennials/#439356e113b8.

Mulhere, Kaitlin. 2018. "This Map Shows the Average Cost of Living in Every State—and What It's Really Worth." *Money*. Updated March 15, 2018. https://money.com/average-income-every-state-real-value/.

Musu, Lauren, Anlan Zhang, Ke Wang, Jizhi Zhang, and B. A. Oudekerk. 2019. *Indicators of School Crime and Safety: 2018*. bjs.gov. https://www.bjs.gov/content/pub/pdf/iscs18.pdf.

Musu-Gillette, Lauren, Rachel Hansen, Kathryn Chandler, and Tom Snyder. 2015. "Measuring Student Safety: Bullying Rates at School." *NCES Blog* (blog), May 1, 2015. https://nces.ed.gov/blogs/nces/post/measuring-student-safety-bullying-rates-at-school.

National Center for Education Statistics. n.d.a. "School Crime and Safety." Updated May 2020. https://nces.ed.gov/programs/coe/indicator_cld.asp.

National Center for Education Statistics. n.d.b. "Table 204.10 Number and Percentage of Public School Students Eligible for Free or Reduced-Price Lunch by State: Selected Years 2000-01 through 2015-16." https://nces.ed.gov/programs/digest/d16/tables/dt16_204.10.asp.

National Center for Education Statistics. n.d.c. "Table 211.60 Estimated Average Annual Salary of Teachers in Public Elementary and Secondary Schools, by State: Selected Years, 1969-70 through 2016-17." https://nces.ed.gov/programs/digest/d17/tables/dt17_211.60.asp.

National Center for Education Statistics. n.d.d. "Table 233.70 Percentage of Public Schools with Security Staff Present at Least Once a Week, and Percentage of Security Staff Routinely Carrying a Firearm, by Selected School Characteristics: 2005-06 through 2015-16." https://nces.ed.gov/programs/digest/d17/tables/dt17_233.70.asp?current=yes.

National Center for Education Statistics. 2019a. "Children With Disabilities." Updated May 2020. https://nces.ed.gov/programs/coe/indicator_cgg.asp.

National Center for Education Statistics. 2019b. "English Language Learners in Public Schools." Updated May 2020. https://nces.ed.gov/programs/coe/indicator_cgf.asp.

National Center for Education Statistics. 2019c. "School Safety and Safety Measures." https://nces.ed.gov/fastfacts/display.asp?id=334.

National Center on Education and the Economy (NCEE). n.d. "Finland: Teacher and Principal Quality." http://ncee.org/what-we-do/center-on-international-education-benchmarking/top-performing-countries/finland-overview/finland-teacher-and-principal-quality/.

National Commission on Excellence in Education. 1983. *A Nation at Risk: The Imperative for Education Reform*. https://www.edreform.com/wp-content/uploads/2013/02/A_Nation_At_Risk_1983.pdf.

National Insurance Institute of Israel. n.d. "Maternity Allowance: Period of Entitlement." https://www.btl.gov.il/English%20Homepage/Benefits/Maternity%20Insurance/Maternity%20Allowance/Pages/Maximum.aspx.

New York City Department of Education. n.d. "2017-18 School Quality Snapshot." https://tools.nycenet.edu/snapshot/2018/.

New York State Education Department. n.d. "Syosset CSD at a Glance." https://data.nysed.gov/profile.php?instid=800000048948.

New York State Education Department. n.d. "Wyandanch UFSD at a Glance." https://data.nysed.gov/profile.php?instid=800000037741.

Organisation for Economic Co-operation and Development. n.d.a. "Income Inequality: OECD Data." https://data.oecd.org/inequality/income-inequality.htm.

Organisation for Economic Co-operation and Development. n.d.b. "Percent of Gross Domestic Product and Monetary Expense in US Dollars for Primary to Post-Secondary, Non-tertiary: OECD Data." https://data.oecd.org/eduresource/public-spending-on-education.htm.

Organisation for Economic Co-operation and Development. n.d.c. "PISA 2018." http://www.oecd.org/pisa/.

Organisation for Economic Co-operation and Development. n.d.d. "Poverty Rate." https://data.oecd.org/inequality/poverty-rate.htm#indicator-chart.

Paltrow, Scot J. 2020. "U.S. Schools Lay Off Hundreds of Thousands, Setting Up Lasting Harm to Kids." *Yahoo News*. Published June 4, 2020. https://www.yahoo.com/news/u-schools-lay-off-hundreds-210156332.html.

Parlapiano, Alicia, and Gregor Aisch. 2017. "Who Wins and Loses in Trump's Proposed Budget." *New York Times*. Updated March 16, 2016. https://www.nytimes.com/interactive/2017/03/15/us/politics/trump-budget-proposal.html.

PBIS Rewards. n.d. "What Is PBIS?" https://www.pbisrewards.com/about.

Pew Research Center. 2019. "Why Americans Don't Fully Trust Many Who Hold Positions of Power and Responsibility." Published September 19, 2019. https://www.people-press.org/2019/09/19/why-americans-dont-fully-trust-many-who-hold-positions-of-power-and-responsibility/.

"Quality Counts 2018: Report and Rankings: A Report Card for States and the Nation on K-12 Education." 2019. *Education Week*. Published June 20, 2018. https://www.edweek.org/ew/collections/quality-counts-2018-state-grades/index.html.

Redding, Christopher. 2018. "Teacher Turnover Is a Problem—Here's How to Fix It." *The Conversations*, University of Florida News. Published September 11, 2018. https://news.ufl.edu/articles/2018/09/teacher-turnover-is-a-problem--heres-how-to-fix-it.html.

Rickenbrode, Robert, Drake Graham, Laura Pomerance, and Kate Walsh. 2018. *Teacher Prep Review*. National Council on Teacher Quality. Published April 2018. https://www.nctq.org/dmsView/2018_Teacher_Prep_Review_733174.

Riggs, Liz. 2013. "Great Teachers Don't Always Want to Become Principals." *The Atlantic* Published November 18, 2013. https://www.theatlantic.com/education/archive/2013/11/great-teachers-dont-always-want-to-become-principals/281483/.

Salary.com. 2020. "School Principal Salary in the United States." https://www.salary.com/research/salary/benchmark/school-principal-salary.

Santoro, Dorris A. 2020. "The Problem with Stories about Teacher Burnout." *Kappan* 101, no. 4 (December/January): 26–33.

Schaffer, Katherine. 2019. "About One-in-Six U.S. Teachers Work Second Jobs—and Not Just in the Summer." *Pew Research Center*. Published July 1, 2019. https://www.pewresearch.org/fact-tank/2019/07/01/about-one-in-six-u-s-teachers-work-second-jobs-and-not-just-in-the-summer/.

Scholastic. n.d. "Teachers Work Nearly 11 Hour Days." https://www.scholastic.com/teachers/articles/teaching-content/teachers-work-nearly-11-hour-days/.

Sedlak, A. J., J. Mettenburg, M. Basena, I. Petta, K. McPherson, A. Greene, and S. Li. 2010. "Fourth National Incidence Study of Child Abuse and Neglect (NIS–4)." Published January 2010. https://cap.law.harvard.edu/wp-content/uploads/2015/07/sedlaknis.pdf.

Simon, Nicole S., and Susan Moore Johnson. 2015. "Teacher Turnover in High Poverty Schools: What We Know and Can Do." *Teachers College Record* 117, no. 3: 1–36. https://www.tcrecord.org/Content.asp?ContentId=17810.

Soffen, Kim, and Denise Lu. 2017. "What Trump Cut in His Budget." *Washington Post*. Updated May 23, 2017. https://www.washingtonpost.com/graphics/politics/trump-presidential-budget-2018-proposal/?utm_term=.6a0c404a100e.

Strauss, Valerie. 2017a. "Where Have All the Teachers Gone?" *Washington Post*. Published September 18, 2017. https://www.washingtonpost.com/news/answer-sheet/wp/2017/09/18/where-have-all-the-teachers-gone/.

Strauss, Valerie. 2017b. "Why It's a Big Problem That So Many Teachers Quit—and What to Do About It." *Washington Post*. Published November 27, 2017. https://www.washingtonpost.com/news/answer-sheet/wp/2017/11/27/why-its-a-big-problem-that-so-many-teachers-quit-and-what-to-do-about-it/.

Stuart, Hunter. 2014. "The Percentage of Americans Who Can't Afford Food Hasn't Budged Since the Recession Peaked." *Huffington Post*. Updated December 6, 2017. https://www.huffpost.com/entry/american-recession-food-insecurity_n_5681559.

Superville, Denise R. 2018. "Most Principals Like Their Jobs: Here's What Makes Them Change Schools or Quit Altogether." *District Dossier* (blog). August 3, 2018. http://blogs.edweek.org/edweek/District_Dossier/2018/08/principal_job_satisfaction_turnover_tenure.html.

Syosset Central School District Report Card. 2018-2019 Proposed Budget. www.syossetschools.org.

Traub, Frank. 2000. "What No School Can Do." *New York Times Magazine*, January 16, 2000. https://www.nytimes.com/2000/01/16/magazine/what-no-school-can-do.html?auth=login-email&login=email.

Treisman, Rachel. 2019. "Poll: Number of Americans Who Favor Stricter Gun Laws Continues to Grow." *NPR*. Published October 20, 2019. https://www.npr.org/2019/10/20/771278167/poll-number-of-americans-who-favor-stricter-gun-laws-continues-to-grow.

Tsukayama, Hayle. 2014. "Technology: 17 Percent of Americans Still Can't Part with Their Landline." *Washington Post*, February 27, 2014. https://www.washingtonpost.com/business/technology/17-percent-of-americans-still-cant-part-with-their-landline/2014/02/27/3fde908e-9fed-11e3-9ba6-800d1192d08b_story.html.

Tucker, Marc. 2019. *Leading High Performance School Systems: Lessons from the World's Best*. Association for Supervision and Curriculum Development (ASCD) and National Center on Education and Economy (NCEE).

Turkish Laborlaw. 2016. "Maternity Leave in Turkey." Published September 29, 2016. https://turkishlaborlaw.com/news/business-in-turkey/maternity-leave-in-turkey/.

US Census Bureau. n.d. "Percentage of People in Poverty by State Using 2- and 3-Year Averages: 2015-2016 and 2017-2018." https://www.census.gov/data/tables/2019/demo/income-poverty/p60-266.html.

"U.S. Department of Education Proposes Plan to Strengthen Teacher Preparation." 2014. Press Release, November 25, 2014. https://www.ed.gov/news/press-releases/us-department-education-proposes-plan-strengthen-teacher-preparation.

US Department of Health and Human Services. n.d. "United States Adolescent Substance Abuse Facts." Updated May 1, 2019. https://www.hhs.gov/ash/oah/facts-and-stats/national-and-state-data-sheets/adolescents-and-substance-abuse/united-states/index.html.

Walsh, Kenneth T. 2019. "Poll: Majority Favor Gun Control." *U.S. News and World Report*, August 19, 2019. https://www.usnews.com/news/national-news/articles/2019-08-19/poll-majority-favor-gun-control.

"We Asked About School Finance. What Did Districts Say?" 2019. *Education Week*, September 24, 2019. https://www.edweek.org/ew/articles/2019/09/25/we-asked-about-school-finance-what-did.html.

"Why Some States Have Higher Teacher Turnover Rates than Others." 2019. *Graide Network* (blog). https://www.thegraidenetwork.com/blog-all/teacher-turnover-rate-by-state.

Wiggins, G., and J. McTighe. 2005. *Understanding by Design*. 2nd ed. expanded. Alexandria, VA: ASCD.

Will, Madeline. 2020. "Teachers Say They're More Likely to Leave the Classroom Because of Coronavirus." *Education Week Teacher*, June 3, 2020. http://blogs.edweek.org/teachers/teaching_now/2020/06/teachers_say_theyre_more_likely_leave_classroom_because_coronavirus.html?cmp=eml-enl-eu-news2&M=59591300&U=&UUID=fd202f8a015e2a7e014bf95a87cccab0.

"Working in Chile: Maternity Leave." 2015. *Inside Santiago: Expat Living Blog*, May 12, 2015. https://insidesantiago.wordpress.com/category/working-in-chile-job-finding-tips/.

Wyandanch Proposed 2019–2020 Budget. www.wyandanch.k12.ny.us.

"Wyandanch Union Free School District, New York Demographics." 2020. *biggestuscities.com*. Updated January 17, 2020. https://www.biggestuscities.com/demographics/ny/wyandanch-union-free-school-district.

About the Author

Charles A. Bonnici has been an educator for fifty years. He served the children of New York City as a teacher, assistant principal, and principal for thirty-two years. He then spent nine years with Pace University in lower Manhattan. He served as an adjunct instructor of educational leadership and an administrator with various responsibilities, including director of school partnerships. Since 2011, he has been a consultant with the Executive Leadership Institute, mentoring first- and second-year assistant principals and designing and facilitating workshops for school-based leaders. This is his fourth book for Rowman & Littlefield.

www.ingramcontent.com/pod-product-compliance
Lightning Source LLC
Chambersburg PA
CBHW030141240426
43672CB00005B/216